SPANISH
IN 3 MONTHS

Isabel Cisneros

YOUR ESSENTIAL GUIDE TO UNDERSTANDING AND SPEAKING SPANISH

Penguin
Random
House

THIRD EDITION
Series Editor Elise Bradbury
Senior Editor Amelia Petersen
Senior Art Editor Jane Ewart
Managing Editors Christine Stroyan, Carine Tracanelli
Managing Art Editor Anna Hall
Production Editor Robert Dunn
Senior Production Controller Samantha Cross
Jacket Project Art Editor Surabhi Wadhwa-Gandhi
Jacket Design Development Manager Sophia MTT
Art Director Karen Self
Associate Publishing Director Liz Wheeler
Publishing Director Jonathan Metcalf

DK INDIA
Project Art Editor Anjali Sachar
Senior DTP Designer Shanker Prasad
Managing Editor Rohan Sinha
Managing Art Editor Sudakshina Basu

This American Edition, 2022
First American Edition, 1987
Published in the United States by DK Publishing
1745 Broadway, 20th Floor, New York, NY 10019
First published in Great Britain by Hugo's Language Books Limited

Copyright © 1987, 1997, 2003, 2022 Dorling Kindersley Limited
DK, a Division of Penguin Random House LLC
23 24 10 9 8 7 6 5
005–326927–Jan/2022

Written by Isabel Cisneros
Formerly Head of Spanish at The Henley College, Oxon

A catalog record for this book is available from the Library of Congress.
ISBN 978-0-7440-5164-3

DK books are available at special discounts when purchased in bulk for sales
promotions, premiums, fund-raising, or educational use. For details, contact:
DK Publishing Special Markets, 1745 Broadway, 20th Floor, New York, NY 10019
Special Sales@dk.com

Printed and bound in China

www.dk.com

Preface

This edition of *Hugo Spanish in 3 Months* was written by Isabel Cisneros, who has considerable experience in teaching her native tongue to secondary school students, adult beginners, and more advanced learners. The course is designed for people learning at home who want to acquire a good working knowledge of Spanish in a short time. The grammar is presented concisely and clearly, maintaining the Hugo principle of teaching only what is really essential and yet providing a complete introduction to written and conversational Spanish. We strongly encourage you to download the free *DK Hugo in 3 Months* app (see p.4) and to listen to the accompanying audio. This will enable you to learn the distinctive sounds of the Spanish language.

Ideally, you should spend about an hour a day on the course, although there is no hard-and-fast rule on this. Do as much as you feel capable of doing; it is much better to learn a little at a time and to learn that thoroughly.

Before beginning a new section, always spend ten minutes reviewing what you learned the day before. Then, read each new section carefully, ensuring that you have fully understood the grammar, before listening to the audio to learn the pronunciation of sample sentences and new vocabulary. Finally, complete the exercises that accompany each section. Repeat them until the answers come easily. Repetition is vital to language learning. The more often you listen to a conversation or repeat an oral exercise, the faster your listening skills and fluency in speaking the language will improve.

After you've completed all the exercises in a week, move on to the drills at the end and read both the stimulus and response out loud. Work through them line by line and use them as a test to see whether you're ready to move on to the next chapter. In addition to the valuable pronunciation practice and general fluency provided by these drills, they can also be treated as written exercises. The answers are at the back of the book.

Each week of the course finishes with a conversation in everyday Spanish, along with an English translation. We suggest that you listen to the conversations first and then read them aloud and see how closely you can imitate the voices on the recording. Take careful note of the use of idioms and new vocabulary as well as relating the constructions you hear to those you've just learned. The course finishes with a piece of text for reading practice, along with the English translation.

When you've completed the course, you should have a very good understanding of the language—more than sufficient for vacation or business purposes and enough to support you in language validation tests if that is your aim. Remember that it is important to continue expanding your vocabulary by reading in Spanish or watching Spanish films—or visiting a Spanish-speaking country!

We hope you enjoy *Hugo Spanish in 3 Months*, and we wish you success with your studies!

About the audio app

The audio app that accompanies this Spanish course contains audio recordings for all numbered sections, vocabulary boxes, conversations, drills, and some of the exercises. There is no audio for the Reading practice section.

◀✕ When you see this symbol, it indicates that there is no audio for that section.

To start using the audio with this book, go to **www.dk.com/hugo** and download the *DK Hugo in 3 Months* app on your smartphone or tablet from the App Store or Google Play. Then, select Spanish from the list of titles.

Please note that this app is not a stand-alone course. It is designed to be used together with the book to familiarize you with Spanish speech and to provide examples for you to repeat aloud.

Contents

Pronunciation   7

Week 1   13
Articles: the, a, an, some
Gender & plural of nouns
Subject pronouns: I, you, he, etc.
Forms of address: Mr., Mrs., etc.
The verb **tener** (to have)
Forming the negative & questions
Idiomatic uses of **tener**
Exercises, drills & conversations

Week 2   24
Contraction of the article
Possession (e.g., "John's father")
Adjectives: describing things
The verbs **ser** & **estar** (to be)
Exercises & conversations

Week 3   33
Demonstratives: this, that, these, those
Regular verbs
The present participle (-ing form)
Question words: what?, who?, whose?, which?, etc.
Relative pronouns: who, which, that, etc.
Exercises, drills & conversation

Week 4   46
Possessive adjectives: my, your, etc.
Possessive pronouns: mine, yours, etc.
Numbers
The time
Days, months, seasons, dates
Exercises & conversation
Review exercises

Week 5   62
The verb **ir** (to go)
The past participle (-ed form)
The present perfect ("I have done")
Hay ("there is," "there are")
Personal **a**
Direct and indirect object pronouns: me, him, to me, to him, etc.
Order of pronouns ("he gives it to me")
Redundant use of object pronouns
The imperative: polite commands
Exercises, drills & conversation

Week 6   77
Some useful question words
Exclamations
Stem-changing verbs
Reflexive verbs (e.g., "I wash myself")
Reciprocal form ("each other")
Personal pronouns with prepositions
Irregular verbs in the present tense
Idiomatic uses of **hacer**
Impersonal verbs
The verbs **gustar** (to like) and **querer** (to want)
Exercises, drills & conversation

Week 7   90
The imperfect tense ("was doing," "used to do")
The verb **soler**
The past perfect (e.g., "had done")
Some negative words: never, nothing, neither, etc.
Adverbs (e.g., "easily," frequently")
Comparison of adjectives, adverbs and nouns ("more ... than," etc.)
Exercises, drills & conversation
Review exercises

Week 8   108

Shortened adjectives
Adjectives that precede the noun
Three irregular verbs
  (present tense)
Some irregular past participles
The future tense (e.g., "will do")
Irregular verbs in the future tense
The conditional (e.g., "would do")
Irregular verbs in the conditional
Uses of the future and conditional
Verbs with prepositions
Idiomatic uses of **llevar**
  and **hacer**
Exercises, drills & conversation

Week 9   122

The preterite ("I spoke," "I ate")
Imperfect and preterite
  contrasted
The two verbs "to know"
Superlative of adjectives
  (e.g., "biggest")
Superlative of adverbs
The absolute superlative
Use of the neuter article **lo**
Uses of definite and indefinite
  articles
Exercises, drills & conversation

Week 10   138

Different uses of **por** and **para**
The passive and its avoidance
Spelling changes in verbs
Verbs followed by an infinitive
Exercises, drills & conversation
Review exercises

Week 11   158

Uses of the verb **deber**
Saber and **poder**
Present and perfect subjunctive
Uses of the subjunctive

The familiar imperative
Idiomatic uses of **seguir**
  and **valer**
Exercises, drills & conversation

Week 12   173

Imperfect and past perfect
  subjunctive
Uses of the imperfect and
  past perfect subjunctive
Sequence of tenses
Use of the subjunctive in "if"
  clauses and in main clauses
"May" and "might"
Verbs followed by prepositions
Al followed by the infinitive
Exercises, drills & conversation

Week 13   188

Some important verbs
Más and **menos**
Tan and **tal**
Pero and **sino**
Prepositions
Augmentatives and diminutives
Idiomatic uses of certain verbs
Exercises, drills & conversation
Review exercises

Reading practice   210

Un tour por Europa

Key to exercises   212

Mini-dictionary   235

Spanish–English
English–Spanish

Index   255

Pronunciation

Before you start the course, read the following pronunciation tips. There's no need to learn these by heart—you can refer back to them whenever you need to, and with practice, you'll soon start to become familiar with Spanish sounds. Listen to the audio in the app to hear the Spanish words and phrases at the same time as you read them. Luckily, Spanish is a very phonetic language, so once you're familiar with its sounds, you will always know how to pronounce a new word you come across.

STRESS

In Spanish, the following rules apply:

1 In most words ending in a vowel, **n** or **s**, the stress is on the next-to-last syllable:
ex*a*men, fl*o*res, h*o*mbre, cigarr*i*llo

2 In most words ending in a consonant other than **n** or **s**, the stress is on the last syllable:
pap*e*l, ciud*a*d, muj*e*r, capit*a*l

3 Exceptions to these two rules are indicated by a written accent on the stressed syllable:
árbol, lámpara, estación, inglés, música

4 The written accent is also used to distinguish words that have the same spelling but different meanings:
el (the), **él** (he); **si** (if), **sí** (yes); **mi** (my), **mí** (me); **mas** (but), **más** (more)

5 The vowels **a, e,** and **o** are strong vowels; **i** and **u** are weak vowels. When two strong vowels occur together, they are pronounced separately:
p*a*ella, te*a*tro, po*e*ta

When two weak vowels occur together, the stress is on the last vowel:
cu*i*da, vi*u*da

When a strong and a weak vowel occur together, the strong vowel is stressed, unless the weak vowel has an accent:
aire, jaula, oído, aún

In the "imitated pronunciation" phonetic transcriptions (see p.12), we show which syllable is stressed by marking ' in front of it.

PRONUNCIATION OF VOWELS

The Spanish vowels are **a, e, i, o,** and **u**. Each vowel has only one sound; this is not quite so long and broad as the English equivalent given below. The vowel sounds are also shortened, as in other languages, when they occur in an unstressed word or syllable or precede a consonant.

a   is pronounced like "ah" in English:
        al (to), **la** (the), **casa** (house)

e   is pronounced like "ay":
        me (me), **de** (from), **le** (him)

i   is pronounced like "ee":
        mi (my), **prima** (cousin)

o   is pronounced like "oh":
        lo (the), **no** (no), **gato** (cat)

u   is pronounced like "oo":
        tu (your), **su** (their), **uno** (one)

PRONUNCIATION OF CONSONANTS

Only two Spanish consonants are pronounced very differently than their English counterparts: **z** and **j**. But several others vary in lesser ways. Here is an overview:

z   is pronounced like "th" in "month" or "thick":
        voz, luz, paz, vez, zapato

j   is pronounced like the German guttural "ch," as in "auch,"
        or like "ch" in the Scottish "loch." This sound is merely
        the English h pronounced in the throat: if you find it hard
        to make, simply pronounce it like an aspirated h:
        ojo, jugar, juzgar, caja

ch is pronounced as in "cheap" or "much":
mucho

c before **e** or **i** is pronounced like the Spanish **z**:
cena, cinco, once

g before **e** or **i** is pronounced like the Spanish **j**:
coger, general, gigante

g before any other letter is like g in "go":
gato

gu before **e** or **i** is like g in "go"; before any other vowel, it
is like "gw-" or "goo":
guerra, guía

h is not pronounced at all:
hijo, hablar

ll is pronounced like y in "yes":
calle, silla, llamar

ñ is like "ny-" in "companion":
niño, señor

qu is like an English k:
que, quince

r is rolled on the tip of the tongue, especially at the
beginning of a word or syllable:
raro

s is always pronounced as in "see" or "last," never
like an English z sound as in "easy" or "miser":
casa, mesa

y as a consonant is like y in "yes": **yo**. But alone or at the
end of a word, it is like the Spanish vowel **i** ("ee"):
y, soy

REGIONAL PRONUNCIATIONS

The lisping pronunciation of **z**, and of **c** before **e** or **i**, is usual in Castile; as Castilian is considered "standard" Spanish, this is the pronunciation we give in this course. But if you travel to different regions, you will hear variations. In Central and South America (and in some parts of Spain), it is usual to pronounce **z**, and **c** before **e** or **i**, like the English s.

Many Spaniards pronounce the final **d** like "th" in "thin" or "myth"; some pronounce **d** in the middle of a word like "th" in "then." But in standard Spanish, **madre** is pronounced ['mah-dray], not ['mah-thray]. A final **d** should not be made too sharp or distinct.

It is also not unusual for Spaniards to pronounce **v** as **b**, so that **vaca** sounds like "baca," for example. This audio for the course includes this pronunciation—see the note in section 3.3.

The letter **ll** is pronounced in several ways, depending on the region: we imitate it as [y], but in some areas of Spain and in Latin America, it can have a strong guttural sound. In the Spanish province of Andalusia and in Argentina, there is an initial sound, something like a soft j or the "zhuh" in "occasion." Thus **mantilla**, which in this course is transcribed as [mahn-'tee-yah], becomes [mahn-'tee-jyah] or [mahn-'tee-zhyah].

PUNCTUATION AND ACCENTS

One thing that can surprise English speakers learning Spanish is that question marks and exclamation points are placed at both ends of the phrase, with the first one inverted.

In terms of accents, **u** becomes **ü** when preceded by **g**, to show that the **u** must be pronounced: **agüero**. The tilde (~) is placed over **n** to show a letter pronounced like "nyuh" in "onion": **mañana**. The use of the acute accent (´) in Spanish is explained on p.7. It never alters the pronunciation of a letter. It is also used in such words as **cuándo** (when) and **dónde** (where) when they are question words: **¿Cuándo llega el buque?** (When does the boat arrive?), BUT **Me alegra cuando llega el buque** (I am glad when the boat arrives).

THE SPANISH ALPHABET

The alphabet consists of 29 letters, of which **K** and **W** are found only in words borrowed from other languages. Note the letters **CH**, **LL**, and **Ñ**. In Spanish dictionaries, words beginning with any one of these will be listed separately—for example, you will not find a word beginning with **CH** by looking under **C**. These letters occur in dictionaries in the order shown below, with **CH** coming after **C, LL** after **L**, and **Ñ** after **N**. Below, the way you say each letter is given according to our system of imitated pronunciation (see p.12).

A	(ah)
B	(bay)
C	(thay)
CH	(chay)
D	(day)
E	(ay)
F	('eff-ay)
G	(Hay)
H	('ah-chay)
I	(ee)
J	('Ho-tah)
K	(kah)
L	('ell-ay)
LL	('ay-yay)
M	('emm-ay)
N	('enn-ay)
Ñ	('enn-yay)
O	(o)
P	(pay)
Q	(koo)
R	('airr-ay)
S	('ess-ay)
T	(tay)
U	(oo)
V	('oo-vay)
W	('oo-vay-'do-blay)
X	('ay-keess)
Y	(ee-gre-'ay-gah)
Z	('thay-tah)

THE "IMITATED PRONUNCIATION"

For the first four weeks, we provide the phonetic transcriptions of each new word. In these transcriptions, the Spanish sounds are represented by English syllables; read these as if each syllable were part of an English word, and you should start to be able to imitate the Spanish sounds, especially if you bear in mind the precisions below:

th   (printed in bold) should be pronounced like "th" in "thin," never as in "they."

H   (printed as a capital letter) should be pronounced gutturally, like "ch" in the Scottish "loch" or German "auch."

s   is always like "ss" in "missing," never like "s" in "easy."

ah   represents the Spanish **a**; this sounds like "ah" in "father," but is a bit shorter. It is never like the "a" in "hat," but remember to keep it short and sharp.

o   resembles the sound of "oh" in "no," although it is not quite as long. It is never like the "o" in "hot."

Week 1

■ *how to say "the," "a," and "some"*
■ *how to recognize whether a noun is masculine or feminine and which article to use with each gender*
■ *forming the plural*
■ *how to say "I," "you," "he," "she," "it," "we," "they"*
■ *forms of address: Mr., Mrs., etc.*
■ *forming the negative and questions*
■ *the present tense of* **tener** *("to have")*

1.1 ARTICLES: THE, A, AN, SOME

In Spanish, articles ("the," "a," etc.) need to agree in gender and number with the noun they precede. If the noun is masculine and singular, the preceding article must also be masculine singular; if the noun is feminine and plural, the article must be feminine plural (indicated by "m. s.," "f. pl.," etc., below). The different forms of the definite article "the" are:

el (m. s.)	**el libro**	the book
la (f. s.)	**la casa**	the house
los (m. pl.)	**los libros**	the books
las (f. pl.)	**las casas**	the houses

The forms of the indefinite article "a," "an," "some" are:

un (m. s.)	**un libro**	a book
una (f. s.)	**una casa**	a house
unos (m. pl.)	**unos libros**	(some) books
unas (f. pl.)	**unas casas**	(some) houses

NOTE: The masculine article is used before a feminine singular noun beginning with **a** or **ha**, if the **a** or **ha** is the stressed vowel:

el agua water
el hambre hunger

IMITATED PRONUNCIATION

ell 'lee-bro; lah 'kah-sah; los lee-bros; lahs 'kah-sahs;
oon 'lee-bro; 'oo-nah 'kah-sah; 'oo-nos 'lee-bros;
'oo-nahs 'kah-sahs; ell 'ah-goo'ah; ell 'ahm-bray

1.2 GENDER OF NOUNS

All Spanish nouns are either masculine or feminine.
There are no neuter nouns. Most nouns ending in -**o** are
masculine. Most nouns ending in -**a, -ión, -d, -z** are
feminine. There are some exceptions, however:

la mano (f.) hand
el camión (m.) truck
el lápiz (m.) pencil
el policía (m.) policeman

Several words ending in -**a** (of Greek origin) are masculine:

el idioma language
el mapa map

Nouns ending in other letters can be either gender:

el hombre man
la mujer woman
la leche milk
el color color

IMITATED PRONUNCIATION

lah 'mah-no; ell kah-mee-'on; ell 'lah-pith;
ell po-lee-'thee-ah; ell ee-dee-'o-mah; ell 'mah-pah;
ell 'om-bray; lah moo-'Hairr; lah 'lay-chay; ell ko-'lorr

PLURAL OF NOUNS

The plural of nouns is formed by adding **-s** to nouns ending in a vowel and **-es** to nouns ending in a consonant:

hombre (man)→ **hombres** (men)
mujer (woman)→ **mujeres** (women)

The plural of nouns ending in **z** is formed by changing the **z** into **c** and adding **-es**:

lápiz (pencil)→ **lápices** (pencils)
luz (light)→ **luces** (lights)

Nouns ending in a consonant in which there is an accent on the last syllable lose that accent when the plural is formed:

camión (truck)→ **camiones** (trucks)

IMITATED PRONUNCIATION

'om-brace; moo-'Hairr-ace; 'lah-pi**th**-ace; loo**th**;
'loo**th**-ace; kah-mee-'on-ace

Exercise 1

Form the plural of:

1	el libro (book)	**7**	el jardín (garden)
2	la casa (house)	**8**	el coche (car)
3	la mujer (woman)	**9**	la capital (capital)
4	el hombre (man)	**10**	la ciudad (city, town)
5	la calle (street)	**11**	la luz (light)
6	la flor (flower)	**12**	la ley (law)

IMITATED PRONUNCIATION

5 'kah-yay; 6 florr; 7 Harr-'deen; 8 'ko-chay;
9 kah-pee-'tahl; 10 **th**e'oo-'dahd; 12 'lay'e

Exercise 2

Put the appropriate definite article before the following nouns:

1 … libros (m., books)
2 … vino (m., wine)
3 … mesas (f., tables)
4 … cerveza (f., beer)
5 … pez (m., fish)
6 … árboles (m., trees)
7 … padre (m., father)
8 … madre (f., mother)
9 … lápiz (m., pencil)
10 … estaciones (f., stations)
11 … billete (m., ticket)
12 … tren (m., train)

Repeat the above exercise using the indefinite article.

IMITATED PRONUNCIATION

'vee-no; 'may-sahs; **th**airr-'vay-**th**ah; pe**th**; 'arr-bol-ace; 'pah-dray; 'mah-dray; 'lah-pi**th**; ess-tah-thee-'on-ace; bee-'yay-tay; trren

Exercise 3

Translate:

1 the book
2 the table
3 the tickets
4 some trees
5 a beer
6 the car
7 a city
8 some lights
9 the garden
10 a street
11 some women
12 the station

SUBJECT PRONOUNS: I, YOU, HE, SHE, ETC.

singular

yo	I
tú	you (fam.)
él, ella	he/she
usted	you (pol.)

plural

nosotros (m.), nosotras (f.)	we
vosotros (m.), vosotras (f.)	you (fam.)
ellos (m.), ellas (f.)	they
ustedes	you (pol.)

In Spanish, there are two different registers to address someone: the familiar **tú** (sing.) and **vosotros/as** (pl.) or the formal **usted** (sing.) and **ustedes** (pl.). The latter are usually written as **Vd./Vds.** or **Ud./Uds.**—they must always be used with the third person verb tense. **Usted** is in fact a contraction of the archaic form of address **Vuestra Merced**, "your honor."

The familiar form is becoming increasingly common in Spain. Some people use it with almost everyone in all circumstances: a professor with students, two people who don't know each other, etc. But others prefer **usted** as a form of courtesy. It is still advisable to use the polite form when addressing strangers, older people, or someone with whom you wish to establish a formal register. The best thing is to be aware of both usages and pay close attention to how someone addresses you to decide which one applies in a given situation.

Note that, unlike in English, subject pronouns are usually omitted, except to give emphasis or avoid ambiguity. This is because the verb conjugation indicates the subject.

IMITATED PRONUNCIATION

yo; too; ell; 'ay-yah; oos-'ted; nos-'otros; nos-'o-trahs; vos-'o-tros; vos-'o-trahs; 'ay-yos; 'ay-yahs; oos-'tay-dace

1.5 FORMS OF ADDRESS: MR., MRS., ETC.

The titles **señor** (sir/Mr.), **señora** (madam/Mrs./Ms.), and **señorita** (Miss) are used to address people whose name is not known. They are used in front of the person's family name, and **señorita** can be employed in front of the person's first name. These titles are always preceded by the definite article, except when used to address the person directly. When used in front of a family name, they are usually written in abbreviated form as: **Sr., Sra., Srta.**

¿Un café, señor?	Coffee, sir?
El Sr. Martínez	Mr. Martínez
La Sra. Martínez	Ms. Martínez
La Srta. Martínez	Miss Martínez
Por aquí, Sr. Martínez.	This way, Mr. Martínez.

The titles **don** and **doña**, for which there are no equivalents in English, are used in formal situations and go in front of the person's first name (without a capital): **don Juan; doña María**.

IMITATED PRONUNCIATION

say-n''yorr; say-n''yor-rah; say-n'yor-'ree-tah; kah-'fay; marr-'tee-ne**th**; porr ah-'kee; don Hoo''ahn; 'don-yah mah-'rree-ah

1.6 THE VERB **TENER** (TO HAVE, TO POSSESS)

This is an irregular verb, and one of the most common, so the sooner you learn it, the better!

present tense

tengo	I have
tienes	you have
tiene	he/she/it has, you have (polite form)
tenemos	we have
tenéis	you have (pl.)
tienen	they have, you have (polite form)

Tienen una hija. They have a daughter.
Tenemos un coche. We have a car.

IMITATED PRONUNCIATION

tay-'nairr; 'ten-go; tee-'ay-nace; tee-'ay-nay;
tay-'nay-mos; tay-'nay-eess; tee-'ay-nen; 'ee-Hah

1.7 FORMING THE NEGATIVE

The negative is formed by putting the word **no** in front
of the verb:

No tengo dinero. I have no money.
No tienen cerveza. They don't have (any) beer.

1.8 FORMING QUESTIONS

The interrogative "Do?" doesn't exist in Spanish. A
question is formed by putting the subject after the verb:

Vd. tiene una pluma. You have a pen.
¿Tiene Vd. una pluma? Do you have a pen?

But a sentence can also be turned into a question simply
by changing the intonation. Note that an inverted question
mark is placed at the beginning of a written question.

1.9 IDIOMATIC USES OF **TENER**

There are a number of idioms with **tener** followed by a
noun when English usually has "to be" followed by an
adjective. Here are some examples:

tener ... años	to be ... years old
tener calor	to be hot
tener cuidado	to be careful
tener en cuenta	to bear in mind

tener éxito	to be successful
tener frío	to be cold
tener ganas de	to feel like, to want to
tener gracia	to be funny
tener hambre	to be hungry
tener miedo	to be afraid
tener paciencia	to be patient
tener prisa	to be in a hurry
tener que hacer	to have things to do
tener que ver con	to have to do with
tener razón	to be right
tener sed	to be thirsty
tener sueño	to be sleepy
tener suerte	to be lucky

When **tener que** is followed by an infinitive, it translates as "to have to," "must":

Tengo que salir. I have to go out.
Tenemos que ver la iglesia. We must see the church.

IMITATED PRONUNCIATION

'ah-n'yos; kah-'lor; koo'ee-'dah-do; en koo-'en-tah;
'ex-ee-to; 'free-o; 'gah-nas day; 'grah-**th**ee-ah;
'ahm-bray; mee-'ay-do; pah-**th**ee-'en-**th**ee-ah; 'pree-sah;
kay ah-'**th**airr; kay vairr kon; rrah-'**th**on; sayd;
soo''ay-n'yo; soo''air-tay; tay-'nairr kay; sah-'leerr;
vairr; ee-'glay-see-ah

As you work through the course, your vocabulary will steadily be increased as you learn new words in the example sentences that illustrate grammar explanations. The vocabulary lists before the exercises show any words in the following exercise that you haven't seen yet, in the order they appear. Read through them before you begin. The adjectives are given in their masculine singular form.

VOCABULARY

el café	coffee
trabajar	to work
todo	everything
salir	to go out
el hijo/la hija	son/daughter

IMITATED PRONUNCIATION

kah-'fay; trah-bah-'Harr; 'to-do; sah-'leerr; 'ee-Ho/Ha

Exercise 4

Translate:

1 They have a house.
2 We don't have (any) coffee.
3 The man is afraid.
4 I have to work.
5 Do you (fam. sing.) have a pencil?
6 They are not thirsty.
7 Do you (pol. pl.) have everything?
8 I'm hot.
9 We have to go out.
10 He has a son.

Drill 1

In this and the other drills that follow, first read the example, which gives a stimulus and a response (not necessarily a simple question and answer). The example will show you what you need to do. In this drill, for instance, the stimulus requires a response alternating between the first-person singular and plural.

Example:

¿Tienes una pluma? Do you have a pen?
No, no tengo pluma. No, I don't have (a) pen.

¿Tenéis un lápiz? Do you (pl.) have a pencil?
No, no tenemos lápiz. No, we don't have (a) pencil.

1 ¿Tienes hambre?
2 ¿Tenéis cerveza?
3 ¿Tienes sed?
4 ¿Tenéis calor?
5 ¿Tienes frío?
6 ¿Tenéis los libros?
7 ¿Tenéis los billetes?

CONVERSATION 1

In this exchange, the context is casual, and the speakers use an informal register.

SR. **¿Tienes una cerveza muy fría? Tengo sed.**
SRA. **Sí, claro. Aquí tienes.**
SR. **¿Cuánto es?**
SRA. **Dos euros con cincuenta.**
SR. **Solo tengo un billete de diez euros. ¿Tienes cambio?**
SRA. **Sí que tengo.**
SR. **Gracias. Adiós.**

TRANSLATION 1

MAN	Do you have a very cold beer? I'm thirsty.
WOMAN	Yes, sure. Here you are.
MAN	How much is it?
WOMAN	Two euros fifty.
MAN	I only have a ten euro note. Do you have change?
WOMAN	Yes, I do.
MAN	Thank you. Goodbye.

CONVERSATION 2

SRA.	**Carmen y Luis tienen un piso en la ciudad y una casa en el campo.**
SR.	**¿Tiene la casa un jardín grande?**
SRA.	**Sí, muy grande y muy bonito, con árboles y flores. También tienen un perro y un gato.**

TRANSLATION 2

WOMAN	Carmen and Luis have an apartment in town and a house in the country.
MAN	Does the house have a big garden?
WOMAN	Yes, very big and very pretty, with trees and flowers. They also have a dog and a cat.

Week 2

- contracted forms of articles
- how to express possession (e.g., "John's father")
- some common adjectives and gender and number agreement with the noun they describe
- the difference between **ser** and **estar** (to be)
- uses of **ser** and **estar**

2.1 CONTRACTION OF THE ARTICLE

When the prepositions **a** (to) and **de** (of, from) are followed by the definite article **el**, they contract to **al** and **del**, respectively: **al castillo** (to the castle), **del jardín** (from the garden).

2.2 POSSESSION (E.G., "JOHN'S FATHER")

There is no apostrophe + s in Spanish. Possession must be expressed by the preposition **de**:

el padre de Juan John's father (lit. "the father of John")
el paraguas de la mujer the woman's umbrella

IMITATED PRONUNCIATION

ah, day; ahl kahs-'tee-yo; del Harr-'deen; 'pah-dray; pah-'rrah-goo'ahs

Exercise 1

Translate:

1	to the church	**7**	of the man
2	of the language	**8**	of the city
3	to the car	**9**	to the street
4	to the table	**10**	of the wine
5	of the trees	**11**	to the policeman
6	to the house	**12**	of the station

2.3 ADJECTIVES: DESCRIBING THINGS

In Spanish, an adjective must agree in gender and number with the noun it qualifies. Adjectives ending in -o in the masculine change the -o to -a in the feminine. The plural is formed by adding -s to both genders. Generally, the adjective comes after the noun:

2

el coche blanco	the white car
la casa blanca	the white house
los coches blancos	the white cars
las casas blancas	the white houses

Adjectives ending in -e and most adjectives ending in a consonant have the same form for both masculine and feminine. The plural is formed by adding -s to those ending in -e and -es to those ending in a consonant.

For example:

el lápiz verde	the green pencil
la pared verde	the green wall
los lápices verdes	the green pencils
las paredes verdes	the green walls
un ejercicio fácil	an easy exercise
una lección fácil	an easy lesson
unos ejercicios fáciles	some easy exercises
unas lecciones fáciles	some easy lessons

Exceptions to this rule are:

1 Adjectives of nationality

inglés	English (m.)	**inglesa**	English (f.)
español	Spanish (m.)	**española**	Spanish (f.)

2 Certain adjectives ending in -n and -or

holgazán	lazy (m.)
holgazana	lazy (f.)
trabajador	hard-working (m.)
trabajadora	hard-working (f.)

IMITATED PRONUNCIATION

'blahn-ko; 'blahn-kah; 'blahn-kos; 'blahn-kahs; 'vairr-day;
pah-'reth; 'vairr-dace; pah-'reth-ace; ay-Hairr-'thee-
thee-o; 'fah-theel; leck-thee-'on; ay-Hairr-'thee-thee-os;
'fah-theel-ace; leck-thee-'on-ace; een-'gless; een-'gless-
ah; es-pah-'n'yol; es-pah-'n'yo-lah; ol-gah-'thahn; ol-gah-
'thahn-ah; trah-bah-Hah-'dorr; trah-bah-Hah-'dor-rah

VOCABULARY 1

el periódico	newspaper	**barato**	cheap
la revista	magazine	**largo**	long
interesante	interesting	**alto**	tall
encantador	charming	**alemán**	German
bueno	good	**americano**	American
útil	useful		

IMITATED PRONUNCIATION

pay-rree-'o-dee-ko; rray-'veess-tah; een-tay-ress-'an-tay;
en-kahn-tah-'dorr; boo''ay-no; 'oo-teel; bah-'rah-to;
'lar-go; 'ahl-to; ah-lay-'mahn; ah-mair-ee-'kah-no

Exercise 2

Make the following adjectives agree where necessary:

1 unos hombres (bueno)
2 una mujer (encantador)
3 unos libros (útil)
4 unas flores (blanco)
5 un coche (barato)
6 una calle (largo)
7 unos árboles (alto)
8 unas ciudades (interesante)
9 un periódico (americano)
10 una revista (alemán)

2.4 SER AND ESTAR

There are two verbs that mean "to be" in Spanish: **ser** and **estar**. The following sections explain when to use which. Here are their conjugations in the present tense.

ser	estar	(to be)
soy	**estoy**	I am
eres	**estás**	you are
es	**está**	he/she/it is, you are (pol.)
somos	**estamos**	we are
sois	**estáis**	you are
son	**están**	they are, you are (pol.)

IMITATED PRONUNCIATION

sairr; es-'tahrr; soy; 'eh-ress; ess; 'so-mos; 'so'ees; son; es-'toy; es-'tahs; es-'tah; es-'tah-mos; es-'tah'ees; es-'tahn

2.5 USES OF SER

The verb **ser** is used to express an inherent characteristic or permanent state. For example:

1 Identity

Soy Carmen. I am Carmen.

2 Possession

El perro es de Juan. The dog is John's.

3 Origin

Mis amigos son de Madrid.
My friends are from Madrid.

4 Nationality

Somos ingleses. We are English.

5 Occupation

El padre de María es arquitecto.
Maria's father is an architect.

6 Material of which something is made

El reloj es de oro. The watch is made of gold.

7 Inherent characteristics
Carlos es muy alto. Charles is very tall.

8 Expressions of time

Son las cinco. It is five o'clock.
Hoy es lunes. Today is Monday.

9 Impersonal expressions

Es mejor esperar. It is better to wait.
Es difícil aprender. It is difficult to learn.

Ser is also used with the past participle of another verb
to form the passive voice (see section 10.2 for more
about the passive):

El ladrón es apresado por la policía.
The thief is captured by the police.

IMITATED PRONUNCIATION

'pairr-o; mees ah-'mee-gos; mah-'dree**th**; arr-kee-'teck-
to; rray-'loH; 'o-ro; moo'ee; '**th**een-ko; oy'ee; 'loo-ness;
may-'Horr; ess-pay-'rahrr; de-'fee-**th**eel; ah-pren-'dairr;
lah-'dron; ah-pray-'sah-do; po-lee-'**th**ee-ah

2.6 USES OF ESTAR

The verb **estar** is used to describe a state or condition of something in time or space: that is, things bound by circumstances—the moment, the place, the physical or emotional state, etc. Use it to indicate:

1 Temporary states or conditions
Pedro está enfermo. Pedro is ill.
Estoy cansada. I'm tired.

2 Position/location (whether temporary or permanent)

Carmen está en el salón. Carmen is in the lounge.
Valencia está en España. Valencia is in Spain.

Estar is also used with the present participle of another verb to form the continuous tenses:

Los niños están jugando en el jardín.
The children are playing in the garden.

These basic rules, however, do not cover every situation. There are cases where it is difficult for a learner to decide which verb is the right one to use. For instance, it could be argued that to be young (**joven**) or to be rich (**rico**) is a temporary condition, but in both cases, **ser** is used. In the exercise on the following page, an English translation will help you decide whether a sentence conveys a "temporary" or "permanent" state.

IMITATED PRONUNCIATION

en-'fairr-mo; sah-'lonn; vah-'len-**th**ee-ah; ess-'pah-n'yah; 'nee-n'yos; Hoo-'gahn-do; 'Ho-ven; 'rree-ko

Exercise 3

Write these sentences in Spanish, with the appropriate form of "ser" or "estar" where these have been omitted.

1 Las lecciones ... difíciles.

The lessons are difficult.

2 El café ... frío.

The coffee is cold.

3 Las chicas ... alemanas.

The girls are German.

4 Jaime ... muy inteligente.

Jaime is very intelligent.

5 Los libros ... sobre la mesa.

The books are on the table.

6 Ana ... triste.

Ana is sad.

7 La mujer de Luis ... abogada.

Luis's wife is a lawyer.

8 La casa ... pequeña.

The house is small.

9 El coche no ... en el garaje.

The car is not in the garage.

10 Yo ... contento con el hotel.

I am pleased with the hotel.

VOCABULARY 2

italiano	Italian	**la colina**	hill
la manzana	apple	**peligroso**	dangerous
en	in, on	**fumar**	to smoke
la cocina	kitchen	**demasiado**	too much
el autobús	bus	**dulce**	sweet
allí	there	**mañana**	tomorrow
la capital	capital	**domingo**	Sunday
España	Spain	**la playa**	beach

IMITATED PRONUNCIATION

'chee-kahs; 'so-bray; 'treess-tay; ah-bo-'gah-dah;
pay-'kay-n'yah; gah-'rrah-Hay; con-'ten-to; con;
ee-tah-lee-'ah-no; mahn-'thah-nah; en; ko-'thee-nah;
ah'oo-to-'booss; ah-'yee; kah-pee-'tahl; ess-'pahn-yah;
ko-'lee-nah; pay-lee-'gro-so; foo-'mahrr;
day-mah-see-'ah-do; dool-**th**ay; mah-'n'yah-nah;
do-'meen-go; 'plah-yah

Exercise 4

Translate:

1 She is Italian.
2 The apples are in the kitchen.
3 The bus is over there.
4 Madrid is the capital of Spain.
5 The girl is tall.
6 The house is on the hill.
7 It is dangerous to smoke.
8 The coffee is too sweet.
9 Tomorrow is Sunday.
10 They are on the beach.

CONVERSATION 1

JUAN **¿Dónde está tu madre?**
TERESA **Está en el jardín, tomando el sol y leyendo el periódico.**
JUAN **Y tu padre ¿dónde está?**
TERESA **Está en la cocina haciendo una paella para la comida.**
JUAN **¡Una paella! ¡Qué bien!**

TRANSLATION 1

JUAN Where's your mother?

TERESA She's in the garden soaking up (lit. "taking") the sun and reading the paper.

JUAN And your father, where's he?

TERESA He's in the kitchen making a paella for lunch.

JUAN Paella! How lovely!

CONVERSATION 2

RECEPCIONISTA **¿Es Vd. la señora García?**

SRA. GARCÍA **Sí.**

RECEPCIONISTA **Tengo un paquete para Vd.**

SRA. GARCÍA **¿De dónde es el paquete?**

RECEPCIONISTA **Es de Los Ángeles.**

SRA. GARCÍA **¡Ah! Muchas gracias.**

RECEPCIONISTA **De nada.**

TRANSLATION 2

RECEPTIONIST Are you Ms. García?

MS. GARCÍA Yes.

RECEPTIONIST I have a package for you.

MS. GARCÍA Where is the package from?

RECEPTIONIST It's from Los Angeles.

MS. GARCÍA Oh! Thank you.

RECEPTIONIST Not at all.

2

Week 3

- *demonstrative adjectives and pronouns ("this," "that," "these," "those")*
- *present tense of regular verbs ending in **-ar, -er, -ir***
- *use of the present participle (the "-ing" form)*
- *question words ("what?," "who?," "whose?," etc.)*
- *relative pronouns ("who," "which," "that," "of whom," etc.)*

3.1 DEMONSTRATIVE ADJECTIVES: THIS, THAT, THESE, THOSE

	masculine	feminine
this	**este**	**esta**
that	**ese**	**esa**
that (over there)	**aquel**	**aquella**
these	**estos**	**estas**
those	**esos**	**esas**
those (over there)	**aquellos**	**aquellas**

Demonstrative adjectives always precede the noun and must agree with it in gender and number:

este coche	this car
esa iglesia	that church
aquellos niños	those children (over there)

A demonstrative adjective cannot be used before one noun and omitted (because implied) before another. It must be repeated:

estos niños y estas niñas	these boys and girls
esas mesas y esas sillas	those tables and chairs

VOCABULARY 1

caro	expensive
fuerte	strong
muy	very
viejo	old
el/la amigo/a	friend
ocupado	occupied, taken, busy
libre	free
el ascensor	elevator
lleno	full
la uva	grape
agrio	sour

IMITATED PRONUNCIATION

'es-tay; 'ay-say; ah-'kel; 'es-tos; 'ay-sos; ah-'kay-yos;
'es- tah; 'ay-sah; ah-'kay-yah; 'es-tahs; 'ay-sahs;
ah-'kay-yahs; 'kah-ro; foo''air-tay; 'moo'ee; vee-'ay-Ho;
ah-'mee-go/ah; o-koo-'pah-do; 'lee-bray; ahs-**th**en-'sor;
'yay-no; 'oo-vah; 'ah-gree-o

Exercise 1

Translate:

1 That car is expensive.
2 Those men are strong.
3 That church is very old.
4 These friends are from Malaga.
5 This table is taken.
6 That man is free (available).
7 This elevator is full.
8 Those grapes are sour.
9 Those books (over there) are interesting.
10 It's that beach (over there).

3.2 DEMONSTRATIVE PRONOUNS

These have the same forms as demonstrative adjectives. They must agree in gender and number with the noun they replace.

For example:
No es este libro, es aquel.
It isn't this book, it's that one over there.
Estos zapatos son caros y esos son baratos.
These shoes are expensive and those are cheap.

The neuter forms of the pronoun—**esto** (this) and **eso, aquello** (that)—are used to refer to things for which the gender has not been established. These forms have no plural.

¿Qué es esto? What is this?
Eso no es correcto. That is not correct.

Este and **aquel**, with their related forms, translate the English "the latter" and "the former," respectively:

Tienen un hijo y una hija. Esta es médica y aquel es profesor.
They have a son and daughter. She is a doctor and he is a teacher.

VOCABULARY 2

la maleta	suitcase
la galleta	cookie
el pan	bread
el abrigo	coat
el zapato	shoe
el vino	wine
la habitación	room

3

IMITATED PRONUNCIATION

mah-'lay-tah; gah-'yay-tah; pahn; ah-'bree-go;
thah-'pah-to; 'vee-no; ah-bee-tah-**th**ee-'on

Exercise 2

3

Replace the words in parentheses with the correct form of the demonstrative adjective or pronoun:

1 No son (these) libros; son (those ones).

2 No es (that) maleta; es (that one over there).

3 No son (these) galletas; son (those ones).

4 No es (that) pan; es (this one).

5 No es (this) abrigo; es (that one over there).

6 No son (those) zapatos; son (these ones).

7 No es (this) vino; es (that one).

8 No es (that) periódico; es (this one).

9 No son (these) habitaciones; son (those ones).

10 No es (this) coche; es (that one over there).

3.3 REGULAR VERBS

Spanish infinitives (e.g., "to speak") end in either **-ar, -er,** or -**ir** (e.g., **hablar, comer, vivir**). Most tenses are formed by removing this ending and adding a specific conjugation ending to the stem. Here are the regular present tense conjugations for these types of verbs:

hablar	comer	vivir
to speak	to eat	to live
habl**o**	com**o**	viv**o**
habl**as**	com**es**	viv**es**
habl**a**	com**e**	viv**e**
habl**amos**	comemos	viv**imos**
habl**áis**	com**éis**	viv**ís**
habl**an**	com**en**	viv**en**

No hablo ruso.	I don't speak Russian.
¿Habla (Vd.) español?	Do you speak Spanish?
Come mucho pan.	He eats a lot of bread.
No comen en el hotel.	They don't eat in the hotel.
¿(Vosotros) vivís aquí?	Do you live here?
Vivo en Londres.	I live in London.

VOCABULARY 3

comprar	to buy
beber	to drink
escribir	to write
estudiar	to study
aprender	to learn
subir	to go up, to bring up

IMITATED PRONUNCIATION

ah-'blahrr; 'ah-blo; 'ah-blahs; 'ah-blah; ah-'blah-mos;
ah-'blah-ees; 'ah-blahn; ko-'mairr; 'ko-mo; 'ko-mes;
'ko-may; ko-'may-mos; ko-'may-ees; 'ko-men; ve-'veerr;
'vee-vo; 'vee-ves; 'vee-vay; ve-'vee-mos; ve-'vees;
'vee-ven; 'rroo-so; 'moo-cho; 'lon-dress; kom-'prahrr;
bay-'bairr; ess-kree-'beerr; ess-too-dee-'ahrr;
ah-pren-'dairr; soo-'beerr

If you have the audio, listen to the recording of **vivir**. This
is a good example of the tendency to pronounce **v** as **b**.
This is what you'll hear more often than not in Spain (see
p.10). However, throughout the course, the imitated
pronunciation uses an English v for the Spanish **v**.

Exercise 3

Translate:

1 I buy.
2 He goes up.
3 You (pol. sing.) drink.
4 We write.
5 They learn.
6 I study.
7 You (fam. sing.) speak.
8 She eats.
9 We live.
10 They go up.
11 I learn.
12 He drinks.

Exercise 4

Translate:

1 He buys a newspaper.
2 Does she drink beer?
3 Pedro lives in Barcelona.
4 I write to Conchita.
5 Do you study English?
6 These children learn Spanish.
7 He talks too much.
8 We go up the hill.
9 I speak English.
10 They drink expensive wine.

The present participle of regular verbs is formed by adding **-ando** to the stem of **-ar** verbs and **-iendo** to the stem of **-er** and **-ir** verbs.

For example:
hablar→ **hablando** (speaking)
comer→ **comiendo** (eating)
vivir→ **viviendo** (living)

The verb **estar** conjugated in the present tense + the present participle forms the present continuous (or progressive) tense (e.g., "I am speaking"):

hablar (to speak)	**comer** (to eat)	**vivir** (to live)
estoy hablando	estoy comiendo	estoy viviendo
estás hablando	estás comiendo	estás viviendo
está hablando	está comiendo	está viviendo
estamos hablando	estamos comiendo	estamos viviendo
estáis hablando	estáis comiendo	estáis viviendo
están hablando	están comiendo	están viviendo

Ramón está bebiendo vino.
Ramon is drinking wine.
El gato está subiendo al árbol.
The cat is going up the tree.
Estoy aprendiendo francés.
I am learning French.

The present continuous has a more restricted use in Spanish than in English. It generally indicates an action taking place at the time of speaking. Otherwise, the simple present tense is used.

IMITATED PRONUNCIATION

ah-'blahn-do; ko-mee-'en-do; vee-vee-'en-do; rrah-'mon; bay-bee-'en-do; 'gah-to; soo-bee-'en-do; ah-pren-dee-'en-do; frahn-'**th**ess

3.5 QUESTION WORDS: WHAT?, WHO?, WHOSE?, WHICH?, ETC.

¿Qué? What?
¿Quién? ¿Quiénes? (pl.) Who? Whom?
¿De quién? Whose?
¿Cuál? ¿Cuáles? (pl.) Which? What?

¿Qué comes (tú)? What are you eating?
¿Quién es (Vd.)? Who are you?
¿De quién es esta pluma? Whose pen is this?

¿Cuál de estos trenes va a Valencia?
Which of these trains goes to Valencia?
¿Cuál es el numero?
What is the number?

¿Qué? can sometimes play the role of an adjective:
¿Qué libros desea (Vd.)? Which books do you want?

IMITATED PRONUNCIATION

kay; kee-'en; kee-'en-ess; day kee-'en; koo''ahl;
koo''ahl-ess

3.6 RELATIVE PRONOUNS: WHO, WHICH, THAT, ETC.

1 que (who, which, that)

This can refer to people or things, singular or plural,
subject or object. Preceded by a preposition, **que** refers
only to things.
For example:

La chica que cuida a los niños
The girl who looks after the children
El coche que conduce
The car he drives
La casa en que vivimos
The house in which we live

2 quien, quienes (who, whom)

This refers only to people, subject or object, and is used mainly after prepositions. It is also used after the verb "to be" and a noun or pronoun.

For example:
el profesor con quien estudio
the teacher with whom I study
el hombre para quien trabaja
the man for whom he works
Es él quien tiene la culpa.
It is he who is to blame.
Es María quien tiene que escribir.
It is Maria who has to write.

3 el que, la que, los que, las que, and **el cual, la cual, los cuales, las cuales** (who, whom, which, that)

These can refer to people or things, subject or object, and are generally used after prepositions:

la mujer con la que está hablando
the woman with whom he is speaking
el autobús en el que viajo
the bus in which I travel
los amigos de los cuales hablábamos
the friends of whom we were talking

el que, la que, los que, las que also translate "he who," "she who," "those who," or "the one/ones who":

El que acaba de llegar es su hijo.
The one who has just arrived is his son.
Los que han venido son todos estudiantes.
Those who have come are all students.

4 cuyo, cuya, cuyos, cuyas (whose, of whom, of which)

These are relative adjectives and agree with the noun they qualify.

el hombre cuya hija es actriz
the man whose daughter is an actress
la novela cuyo título no recuerdo
the novel whose title I don't remember

5 lo que/lo cual (what, which) refers to a clause
or an idea

No comprendo lo que dice.
I don't understand what he says.
No ha llegado todavía, lo cual me sorprende.
He hasn't arrived yet, which surprises me.

Note that the relative pronoun can never be omitted in
Spanish (as it often is in English):

El hombre a quien quiero ver
The man (who) I want to see
El periódico que lee
The newspaper (that) he reads

IMITATED PRONUNCIATION

kay; koo''ee-dah; kon-'doo-**th**ay; kee-'en; kee-'en-ess;
pro-fay-'sorr; 'kool-pah; el kay, el koo''ahl etc.;
vee-'ah-Ho; ah-'kah-bah; ess-too-dee-'ahn-tess;
'koo-yah etc.; ac-'tree**th**; no-'vay-lah; 'tee-too-lo;
rray-koo''air-do; lo kay; lo koo''ahl; 'dee-**th**ay;
to-dah-'vee-ah; sorr-'pren-day; kee-'ay-ro vairr; 'lay-ay

VOCABULARY 4

el pueblo	village
la tienda	shop
leer (leyendo)	to read (reading)
el/la médico/a	doctor
la carta	letter
verde	green
la puerta	door
la pluma	pen
con	with
el número	number

IMITATED PRONUNCIATION

poo''ay-blo; tee-'en-dah; lay-'airr; lay-'en-do; 'may-dee-ko/kah; 'kahrr-tah; 'vairr-day; poo''air-tah; 'ploo-mah; kon; 'noo-may-ro

Exercise 5

Translate:

1 The village in which we live
2 The woman who works in the shop
3 The book that I have to read
4 The town of which we are speaking
5 It's Maria who is (a) doctor.
6 Whose letters are these?
7 Which magazine is he buying?
8 The house that has a green door
9 The pen with which I write
10 What is the number?

Drills 1–3

Example:

¿Son (Vds.) americanos? Are you (pl.) American?
Sí, somos americanos. Yes, we're American.

¿Es (Vd.) americana? Are you American?
Sí, soy americana. Yes, I'm American.

1 ¿Beben (Vds.) cerveza?
2 ¿Come (Vd.) pan?
3 ¿Viven (Vds.) en Boston?
4 ¿Es (Vd.) médico?
5 ¿Hablan (Vds.) español?
6 ¿Compra (Vd.) la revista?

Example:

¿Eres inglés? Are you English?
No, no soy inglés. No, I'm not English.

¿Sois ingleses? Are you (pl.) English?
No, no somos ingleses. No, we're not English.

1 ¿Vives en Barcelona?
2 ¿Comprendes?
3 ¿Aprendes alemán?
4 ¿Compras los periódicos?
5 ¿Bebes vino?
6 ¿Sois españoles?

Fill in the gaps with the correct form of the present continuous. Example:
¿Qué come? Está comiendo pan.

1 ¿Qué compra? … el periódico.
2 ¿Qué beben? … cerveza.
3 ¿Qué estudia (Vd.)? … español.
4 ¿Qué comen (Vds.)?… uvas.
5 ¿Qué lee? … una revista.
6 ¿Qué hablan (Vds.)? … inglés.
7 ¿Qué escribe? … una carta.
8 ¿Qué aprenden? … español.
9 ¿Qué sube (Vd.)? … las maletas.

CONVERSATION

En la librería

DEPENDIENTA	**Buenos días, señor. ¿Qué desea?**
CLIENTE	**Buenos días. ¿Tiene Vd. un libro de historia de España?**
DEPENDIENTA	**Sí, señor, tenemos varios. Este es muy bueno, tiene muchas ilustraciones.**
CLIENTE	**Sí, parece muy interesante. ¿Cuánto es?**
DEPENDIENTA	**Veinticinco euros.**
CLIENTE	**Es un poco caro. Y ese ¿cuánto es?**
DEPENDIENTA	**Ese, veinte euros.**
CLIENTE	**Muy bien, ese, por favor.**

TRANSLATION

At the bookshop

SHOP ASSISTANT	Good morning, sir. Can I help you?
CUSTOMER	Good morning. Do you have a book on the history of Spain?
SHOP ASSISTANT	Yes, we have several. This one is very good, it has a lot of illustrations.
CUSTOMER	Yes, it looks very interesting. How much is it?
SHOP ASSISTANT	Twenty-five euros.
CUSTOMER	It's a little expensive. And that one, how much is it?
SHOP ASSISTANT	That one is twenty euros.
CUSTOMER	All right, that one, please.

Week 4

- *possessive adjectives ("my," "your," "his," etc.) and how they agree with the thing possessed, not the possessor*
- *possessive pronouns ("mine," "yours," etc.)*
- *cardinal numbers ("one," "two," etc.)*
- *ordinal numbers ("first," "second," etc.)*
- *expressions of time*
- *dates, months, seasons, and days of the week*

4.1 POSSESSIVE ADJECTIVES: MY, YOUR, ETC.

	singular	plural
my	**mi**	**mis**
your	**tu**	**tus**
his, her, its, your (pol.)	**su**	**sus**
our	**nuestro/a**	**nuestros/as**
your	**vuestro/a**	**vuestros/as**
their, your (pol.)	**su**	**sus**

In Spanish, possessive adjectives agree with the thing possessed, not with the possessor:

mi coche	my car
mis hermanos	my brothers
nuestro perro	our dog
nuestras hijas	our daughters

Although "his," "her," "its," "their," and "your" are all translated by the forms **su** and **sus**, the meaning is usually clear from the context. However, in cases of ambiguity, the following forms can be used: **de él**, **de ella**, **de ellos**, **de ellas**, **de Vd.**, **de Vds.**

For example:

el libro de Vd.	your book
el amigo de ellos	their friend

VOCABULARY 1

el hermano	brother
la hermana	sister
el tío	uncle
la tía	aunt
el marido	husband
la mujer	wife
el primo	cousin (m.)
la prima	cousin (f.)
el sobrino	nephew
la sobrina	niece
los padres	parents
los parientes	relatives

IMITATED PRONUNCIATION

mee; mees; too; toos; soo; sooss, etc.; airr-'mahn-o;
airr-'mahn-ah; 'tee-o; 'tee-ah; mah-'ree-do; moo-'Hairr;
'pree-mo; 'pree-mah; so-'bree-no; so-'bree-nah;
'pah-drace; pah-ree-'en-tace

Exercise 1

Translate:

1 my husband
2 her brother
3 our sister
4 their nephew
5 his uncle
6 my parents
7 your (fam.) wife
8 their sons
9 your (pol. sing.) cousin (m.)
10 his relatives

4.2 POSSESSIVE PRONOUNS: MINE, YOURS, ETC.

	singular	plural
mine	**el mío, la mía**	**los míos, las mías**
yours	**el tuyo, la tuya**	**los tuyos, las tuyas**
his, hers, its, yours (pol.)	**el suyo, la suya**	**los suyos, las suyas**
ours	**el nuestro, la nuestra**	**los nuestros, las nuestras**
yours	**el vuestro, la vuestra**	**los vuestros, las vuestras**
theirs, yours (pol.)	**el suyo, la suya**	**los suyos, las suyas**

Possessive pronouns agree in gender and number with the noun they replace. They are always preceded by the definite article, except after the verb **ser**, when the article is usually omitted.

For example:
mi casa y la tuya my house and yours
Estas cartas son nuestras. These letters are ours.

These forms are also used as adjectives, after the noun and without the article:

1 for emphasis:

¿Cuál es el coche vuestro?
Which is *your* car?

2 for direct address (as in letters):

Muy señor mío Dear sir

3 to translate "of mine," "of yours," etc.:

un amigo mío a friend of mine
una idea suya an idea of his

IMITATED PRONUNCIATION

'mee-o/ah; 'mee-os/ahs; 'too-yo, etc.; 'soo-yo, etc.

Exercise 2

Replace the word in parentheses with the appropriate form of the possessive pronoun:

1 mi casa y (yours, fam. sing.)
2 nuestro jardín y (theirs)
3 su coche y (ours)
4 mi mujer y (his)
5 vuestra madre y (ours)
6 su padre y (mine)
7 mi cerveza y (yours, pol.)
8 nuestros amigos y (yours, fam. pl.)
9 su secretaria y (mine)
10 tu gato y (hers)

4

1	uno (m.), una (f.)	50	cincuenta
2	dos	60	sesenta
3	tres	70	setenta
4	cuatro	80	ochenta
5	cinco	90	noventa
6	seis	100	cien, ciento
7	siete	101	ciento uno/a
8	ocho	102	ciento dos
9	nueve	200	doscientos/as
10	diez	300	trescientos/as
11	once	400	cuatrocientos/as
12	doce	500	quinientos/as
13	trece	600	seiscientos/as
14	catorce	700	setecientos/as
15	quince	800	ochocientos/as
16	dieciséis	900	novecientos/as
17	diecisiete	1,000	mil
18	dieciocho	1,001	mil uno/a
19	diecinueve	1,002	mil dos
20	veinte	1,100	mil cien
21	veintiuno/a	1,101	mil ciento uno/a
22	veintidós	1,200	mil doscientos/as
23	veintitrés, etc.	2,000	dos mil
30	treinta	100,000	cien mil
31	treinta y uno/a	200,000	doscientos mil
32	treinta y dos	1,000,000	un millón
40	cuarenta	2,000,000	dos millones

IMITATED PRONUNCIATION

'oo-no; 'oo-nah; doss; tress; koo''ah-tro; '**th**een-ko;
'say-eess; see-'ay-tay; 'o-cho; noo''ay-vay; dee-'e**th**;
'on-**th**ay; 'do-**th**ay; 'tray-**th**ay; kah-'torr-**th**ay;
'keen-**th**ay; dee-'e**th**-ee-'say-ess, etc.; (20) 'vay'n-tay;
'vay'n-tee-'oo-no, etc.; (30) 'tray-een-tah, etc.;
(40) koo'ah-'ren-tah; **th**een-koo''en-tah; say-'sen-tah;
say-'ten-tah; o-'chen-tah; no-'ven-tah; **th**ee-'en;
thee-'en-to, etc.; (1000) meel; (1,000,000) mee-'yon

Uno and **ciento** are contracted to **un** and **cien** in front of a noun or an adjective:

un libro   one book
cien libros a hundred books

Exercise 3

Translate:

1 ten houses
2 seventy-two euros
3 two hundred women
4 sixteen letters
5 one hundred thirty-five books
6 forty-six hotels
7 three hundred fifty-four apples
8 sixty-eight shops
9 one thousand four hundred men
10 seven hundred eighty-five cars

4.4 ORDINAL NUMBERS: FIRST, SECOND, ETC.

1st	primero	6th	sexto
2nd	segundo	7th	séptimo
3rd	tercero	8th	octavo
4th	cuarto	9th	noveno
5th	quinto	10th	décimo

Beyond "tenth," cardinal numbers are generally used:

Felipe II (segundo)	Philip II
Alfonso XII (doce)	Alfonso XII
el siglo III (tercero)	the 3rd century
el siglo XX (veinte)	the 20th century
el octavo piso	the eighth floor
el piso trece	the thirteenth floor

Note that with titles and centuries, both ordinal and cardinal numbers follow the noun.

All the ordinal numbers form their feminine and plural in the usual way:

la tercera vez the third time
los primeros días the first days

Primero and **tercero** are shortened to **primer** and **tercer** in front of a masculine noun:

el primer hombre the first man
el tercer niño the third child

IMITATED PRONUNCIATION

pree-'may-ro; say-'goon-do; tairr-'**th**ay-ro; koo''ar-to;
'keen-to; 'sex-to; 'sep-tee-mo; ock-'tah-vo; no-'vay-no;
'day-**th**ee-mo; fay-'lee-pay; ahl-'fon-so; 'see-glo; 'pee-so;
ve**th**; 'dee-ahss; pree-'mairr; tairr-'**th**airr

Exercise 4

Translate:

1 the seventh book
2 the first wife
3 the third daughter
4 the sixth son
5 the second door
6 the tenth day
7 the fourth street
8 the ninth child
9 the fifth man
10 the eighth shop

THE TIME

Asking and giving the time is quite easy, but note that the word **hora** (f.) (hour) is used:

¿Qué hora es? What's the time?
Es la una. It's one o'clock.
Son las dos. It's two o'clock.
Son las tres. It's three o'clock.

Note that the feminine article is used because it stands in for **la hora**, and the plural form (for the verb as well as the article) applies in all hours except "one."

"Quarter to" is expressed by **menos cuarto**, "quarter past" by **y cuarto**, and "half past" by **y media**.

For example:
Son las siete y diez. It is ten past seven.
Es la una menos veinte. It is twenty to one.
Son las ocho y media. It is half past eight.
Son las cinco menos cuarto. It is quarter to five.
Son las nueve y cuarto. It is quarter past nine.

Mediodía is "midday," and **medianoche** is "midnight." If you want to be exact, **a las once en punto** means "at eleven o'clock precisely." **A eso de** means "at about ...."

"a.m." is expressed by **de la mañana**, and "p.m." by **de la tarde** or **de la noche** (use the latter for times after around 8:30 p.m.).

For example:
El tren sale a las nueve de la mañana.
The train leaves at 9 a.m.
En España comemos a eso de las dos de la tarde.
In Spain we have lunch at about 2 p.m.
Pedro llega a su casa a las once de la noche.
Peter arrives at his house at 11 p.m.

The expressions **por la mañana** ("in the morning"), **por la tarde** ("in the afternoon," "in the evening"), and **por la noche** ("at night") are used when the time of day is not given:

Ramón trabaja por la mañana.
Ramon works in the morning.
Leo en el jardín por la tarde.
I read in the garden in the afternoon.
Por la noche todo está en silencio.
At night everything is silent.

IMITATED PRONUNCIATION

kay 'o-rah ess; 'may-nos koo''ar-to; ee 'may-dee-ah;
may-dee-o-'dee-ah; may-dee-ah-'no-chay;
mah-n''yah-nah; 'tarr-day; 'no-chay

4.6 DAYS OF THE WEEK & TIME EXPRESSIONS

The days of the week (which in Spanish do not begin with a capital letter) are:

lunes	Monday
martes	Tuesday
miércoles	Wednesday
jueves	Thursday
viernes	Friday
sábado	Saturday
domingo	Sunday

The days of the week are always preceded by the definite article **el**.

For example:
el domingo por la mañana
Sunday morning

Some useful expressions of time:

ayer	yesterday
anteayer	the day before yesterday
hoy	today
hoy día	nowadays
mañana	tomorrow
pasado mañana	the day after tomorrow
mañana por la mañana	tomorrow morning
mañana por la tarde	tomorrow afternoon/evening
mañana por la noche	tomorrow night
de día	by day
de noche	by night
al día siguiente	on the following day
un día sí y otro no	every other day
a los pocos días	a few days later
hace unos días	a few days ago

IMITATED PRONUNCIATION

'loo-ness; 'mar-tess; mee-'air-co-less; Hoo-'ay-vess;
vee-'air-ness; 'sah-bah-do; do-'meen-go; ah-'yair;
ahn-tay-ah-'yair; 'o'ee; 'o'ee 'dee-ah; mah-n''yah-nah;
pah-'sah-do; 'no-chay; se-ghee-'en-tay

4.7 MONTHS OF THE YEAR

The months of the year, which also start with a lower-case letter in Spanish, are:

enero	January	**julio**	July
febrero	February	**agosto**	August
marzo	March	**septiembre**	September
abril	April	**octubre**	October
mayo	May	**noviembre**	November
junio	June	**diciembre**	December

4.8 SEASONS OF THE YEAR

The seasons of the year are:

la primavera   spring
el verano   summer
el otoño   fall
el invierno   winter

Only spring is feminine; the other seasons are all masculine nouns.

IMITATED PRONUNCIATION

ay-'nay-ro; fay-'bray-ro; 'mar-**th**o; ah-'breel; 'mah-yo;
'Hoo-nee-o; 'Hoo-lee-o; ah-'gos-to; sep-tee-'em-bray;
ok-'too-bray; no-vee-'em-bray; dee-**th**ee-'em-bray;
pree-mah-'vay-rah; vay-'rah-no; o-'to-n'yo; in-vee-'air-no

4.9 DATES

The date can be expressed in two ways:

1 with the verb **estar**

¿A cuántos estamos?
What is the date?

2 with the verb **ser**

¿Qué fecha es hoy?
What is the date today?
Estamos a siete *or* **Es el siete.**
It's the seventh ("the 7").

For the first of the month, you can use either the cardinal or ordinal number (use cardinal numbers for the rest):

el uno/primero de mayo
the first of May

el quince de octubre
the 15th ("the 15") of October
[Nació] el cuatro de abril de mil novecientos dos.
[He was born on] 4 April 1902.

VOCABULARY 2

hasta	until
frío	cold
las vacaciones	vacations
el cumpleaños	birthday
generalmente	usually
ir	to go
cenar	to have dinner
el reloj	watch, clock

IMITATED PRONUNCIATION

'fay-chah; nah-**th**ee-'o; 'ahs-tah; 'free-o;
vah-kah-**th**ee-'o-ness; koom-play-'ah-n'yos;
Hay-nay-rahl-'men-tay; eer; **th**ay-'narr; rray-'loH

Exercise 5

Translate:

1 What's the time?
2 It is twenty past ten on my watch.
3 I work until half past eleven.
4 The winter in Madrid is cold.
5 They have their holidays in July.
6 My birthday is (on) the 3rd of January.
7 He is free on Saturdays.
8 October is usually a beautiful month.
9 We have to go to Barcelona in May.
10 On Sundays I have dinner with my parents.

Juan y Carmen trabajan en la misma oficina.

JUAN   **Oye, Carmen, el sábado doy una pequeña fiesta en mi casa.**

CARMEN   **¡Ah, qué bien!**

JUAN   **Es mi cumpleaños y quiero celebrarlo.**

CARMEN   **Así que tu cumpleaños es en junio. El mío también. ¡Qué casualidad!**

JUAN   **¿En qué fecha es el tuyo?**

CARMEN   **El dieciocho.**

JUAN   **Tres días después del mío, entonces. Bueno, ¿puedes venir a mi fiesta?**

CARMEN   **¿A qué hora es?**

JUAN   **A las ocho.**

CARMEN   **Me gustaría, pero el sábado tengo que trabajar horas extraordinarias hasta las nueve y media.**

JUAN   **No te preocupes porque la fiesta dura hasta la una o las dos de la mañana.**

CARMEN   **En ese caso acepto. ¿Has invitado a mucha gente?**

JUAN   **No, doce o catorce amigos, porque mi casa no es muy grande. Hasta el sábado, entonces.**

CARMEN   **Adiós y gracias por invitarme.**

4

TRANSLATION

Juan and Carmen work in the same office.

> JUAN   Listen, Carmen, on Saturday I'm giving
> (lit. "I give") a little party at home.
>
> CARMEN   How nice!
>
> JUAN   It's my birthday and I want to celebrate it.
>
> CARMEN   So, your birthday is in June. Mine too.
> What a coincidence!
>
> JUAN   What date is yours?
>
> CARMEN   The eighteenth.
>
> JUAN   Three days after mine, then. Well, can you
> come to my party?
>
> CARMEN   At what time?
>
> JUAN   At eight o'clock.
>
> CARMEN   I'd like to, but on Saturday I have to work
> overtime until 9:30.
>
> JUAN   Don't worry, because the party will go on
> (lit. "lasts") until one or two in the morning.
>
> CARMEN   In that case, I accept. Have you invited
> many people?
>
> JUAN   No, 12 or 14 friends because my house isn't
> very big. Until Saturday then.
>
> CARMEN   Bye, and thanks for inviting me!

4

Review exercises

Exercise 1

Fill in the blanks, choosing a verb from the column on the right:

1	Solo … un billete de diez euros.	habla
2	Carmen y Pedro … en Barcelona.	aprende
3	Mi hermana … profesora.	son
4	¿Dónde … los periódicos?	cena
5	Los niños no … mucho pan.	viven
6	Es italiano, pero … español.	trabajamos
7	Estos zapatos … muy caros.	es
8	Ramón … generalmente a las nueve.	están
9	Mi primo … francés y alemán.	comen
10	Nosotros no … los sábados.	tengo

Exercise 2

Translate:

1 In Spain, American newspapers are very expensive.
2 Where are the suitcases?
3 The room is on the third floor.
4 In the summer they live in England, and in winter they live in Spain.
5 Her husband is busy; he works too much.
6 I have to write to my German friend (f.).
7 These flowers are for John's mother.
8 Mrs. Suarez is a charming woman.
9 We have to buy the tickets.
10 What's the time? Quarter past seven.
11 Is that dog yours (pol.)?
12 Our daughter is learning Spanish.

Exercise 3

Answer the following questions by translating the sentences shown in English:

1 ¿De dónde eres?
  I am American.

2 Entonces, ¿vives en Washington?
  No, I live in Boston.

3 ¿Por qué estás en España?
  I am on holiday.

4 ¿Cuántas semanas de vacaciones tienes?
  Only two.

5 ¿Trabajas?
  Yes, I work in a shop.

6 ¿Qué clase de tienda?
  It's a bookshop.

7 ¿Estás en un hotel?
  No, I am at a friend's (f.) house.

8 ¿Dónde vive tu amiga?
  In a house on the beach.

9 ¿Tienes sed? ¿Quieres (would you like) una cerveza?
  No, thank you, I'm in a hurry. Goodbye.

Week 5

- *the verb* **ir** *(to go)*
- *the past participle (the -ed form) and the present perfect tense (introducing the auxiliary verb* **haber***)*
- *saying "there is" and "there are"*
- *personal pronouns used as direct and indirect objects ("her," "to her," "him," "to him," etc.)*
- *the imperative*

5.1 THE VERB IR (TO GO)

This very common verb is irregular, and you'll be using it a lot! Its present tense is as follows:

voy	**vamos**
vas	**vais**
va	**van**

To say "to go to" or "to be going to," use **ir a**, e.g.:

Van a la iglesia.
They go to church.
Voy a comprar un periódico.
I'm going to buy a newspaper.

The first-person plural **vamos** translates to "let's" as well as "we go to" and "we are going to" + verb (the near future). The meaning is usually clear from the context:

Vamos al cine todos los viernes.
We go to the movies every Friday.
Vamos a comprar los billetes.
We're going to buy the tickets.
Vamos a ver.
Let's see.

VOCABULARY 1

ir de vacaciones	to go on vacation
por	by
tomar	to have (food or drink)
cantar	to sing
descansar	to rest
ir de compras	to go shopping
el mercado	market
el teatro	theater

Exercise 1

5

Translate:

1 We go to church on Sundays.
2 I'm going to buy that book.
3 He goes to his friend's house.
4 We go on vacation in the summer.
5 They go to Madrid by train.
6 Let's have a coffee.
7 She's not going to sing.
8 Tomorrow I'm going to rest.
9 They go shopping in the market.
10 Let's go to the theater.

5.2 THE PAST PARTICIPLE (-ED FORM)

The past participle of regular verbs is formed by replacing the infinitive ending with **-ado** for **-ar** verbs, or **-ido** for **-er** and **-ir** verbs.

hablar→ **hablado** (talked, spoken)
comer→ **comido** (eaten)
vivir→ **vivido** (lived)

Some verbs have irregular past participles. Here are a few examples of this in some common verbs:

escribir (to write)→ **escrito** (written)
ver (to see)→ **visto** (seen)
hacer (to do, to make)→ **hecho** (done, made)
decir (to say, to tell)→ **dicho** (said, told)

5.3 THE PRESENT PERFECT (E.G., "I HAVE DONE")

The present perfect is formed with the present tense of the auxiliary verb **haber** (to have) followed by the past participle of the main verb. For example, the present perfect of the verb **comprar** (to buy) is:

he comprado	I have bought
has comprado	you have bought
ha comprado	he/she has bought
hemos comprado	we have bought
habéis comprado	you have bought
han comprado	they have bought

Note that **haber** is used only as an auxiliary verb and is never used on its own to mean "to have" (i.e., **tener**).

The use of the present perfect is similar to that in English, but in Spanish, this tense is sometimes used where in English we would use the simple past. So:
Hemos viajado todo el día.
We have traveled all day. *or* We traveled all day.

Note that the auxiliary and the past participle must not be separated in Spanish:

Siempre he trabajado.
I have always worked.

5.4 HAY ("THERE IS," "THERE ARE")

"There is" and "there are" are translated by **hay**, which is an impersonal form of the verb **haber**. Note that **hay** is used for both the singular and the plural:

Hay una barca en la playa.
There is a boat on the beach.
Hay muchos turistas en esta ciudad.
There are many tourists in this town.

The construction **hay que** + infinitive indicates necessity and is usually translated by "one must" or "you must":

Hay que ver la catedral.
You must see the cathedral.
No hay que llorar.
One mustn't cry.

In the present perfect (there has/have been), you use the third-person singular present tense of the verb **haber** plus its past participle **(ha habido)**:

Ha habido un accidente de carretera.
There has been a road accident.
Ha habido muchos problemas.
There have been many problems.

5

VOCABULARY 2

el azúcar	sugar
el té	tea
nuevo	new
el vestido	dress
terminar	to finish
el trabajo	job, work
ayudar	to help
la naranja	orange
la bolsa	bag
la película	movie

Exercise 2

Translate:

1 I have written three letters.
2 They have spoken in Spanish.
3 We have eaten too much.
4 There is sugar in this tea.
5 She has bought a new dress.
6 Have you finished the job?
7 They have never helped in the house.
8 There are some oranges in the bag.
9 Did you (pol. sing.) drink the water?
10 I haven't seen the movie.

5.5 PERSONAL A

All verbs except **tener** are followed by the preposition **a** when the direct object is a definite person or animal:

Llamo a Pedro. I'll call Pedro.
Llamo a mi perro. I'm calling my dog.
but
Tiene un perro. She has a dog.
Compra el libro. He buys the book.

VOCABULARY 3

visitar	to visit
llamar	to call
preparar	to prepare
la comida	meal, food
invitar	to invite
casado/a	married
el caballo	horse
bañar	to bathe
esperar	to wait for, to expect
el profesor / **la profesora**	teacher

Exercise 3

Rewrite the following sentences, filling in the blanks with the personal "a" where necessary:

1 Voy a ver ... mi tío.
2 Tenemos que ayudar ... nuestros amigos.
3 Juan ha comprado ... un perro.
4 No he hablado ... el médico.
5 Está leyendo ... el periódico.
6 Vamos a invitar ... Pedro.
7 Tengo ... tres hermanos.
8 Esperamos ... una carta de María.
9 Voy a beber ... una cerveza.
10 Están llamando ... su hija.

Exercise 4

Translate:

1 He visits his mother.
2 I have seen the woman.
3 We have to call the dogs.
4 Maria prepares the meal.
5 They have invited their friends.
6 She has a married sister.
7 I'm going to buy a horse.
8 We have to bathe the child.
9 They are waiting for the teacher (m.).
10 Carlos has not seen the movie.

5.6 DIRECT AND INDIRECT OBJECT PRONOUNS: ME, HIM, TO ME, TO HIM, ETC.

Direct object pronouns

me	me
te	you (fam.)
lo (le)*	him, you (pol. m.)
la	her, you (pol. f.)
lo, la	it (m.), it (f.)
nos	us
os	you (fam.)
les	you (pol. m.)
las	them, you (pol. f.)
los, las	them (m., f.)

Indirect object pronouns

me	to me
te	to you
le	to him, to her, to it, to you (pol.)
nos	to us
os	to you
les	to them, to you (pol.)

* When the masc. sing. direct object refers to a person (i.e., a man or a boy), you may hear **le** or **lo**: both are accepted.

Object pronouns usually precede the verb:

Nos ayuda con el trabajo. He helps us with the work.
Le he escrito una carta. I have written him a letter.

When the verb is an infinitive, a present participle, or an imperative, the pronoun is usually added to the end of the verb:

Tengo que comprarlo. I have to buy it.
Está esperándome. He is waiting for me.
Bébalo. Drink it.

If the infinitive or present participle is preceded by another verb, as in the case of the examples above, the object pronoun can be placed before that verb (this is optional):

Lo tengo que comprar. I have to buy it.
Me está esperando. He is waiting for me.

When an object pronoun is added to the present participle, an accent must be used so that the stress still falls on the same syllable:

Está bebiéndolo. He is drinking it.
Estamos terminándolo. We are finishing it.

5.7 ORDER OF PRONOUNS ("HE GIVES IT TO ME")

When two object pronouns are used together, the indirect object pronoun always comes first:

Me lo da. He gives it to me.
Nos la lee. She reads it to us.

When two third-person pronouns are used together, the indirect object pronoun **le/les** becomes **se**:

Se la envía. He sends it to him.

In order to avoid any possible ambiguity in the meaning of **le**, **les**, or **se**, you may add **a él**, **a ellas**, or **a Vd.**, after the verb:

Le escribo la carta a él. I write the letter to him.
Les compro flores a ellas. I buy them flowers.
Se lo he dado a Vd. I have given it to you.

5.8 REDUNDANT USE OF OBJECT PRONOUNS

Sometimes, for emphasis, the noun or pronoun that is the direct or indirect object of the sentence precedes the verb. When this happens, the corresponding object pronoun must also be used immediately before the verb.

For example:
A esos amigos los veo poco.
I don't see much of those friends.
A Juan le he comprado una corbata.
For Juan, I have bought a tie.
A nosotros no nos han invitado.
They haven't invited us.

Even when the indirect object noun or pronoun follows the verb, the corresponding object pronoun is often inserted before the verb. This is especially common in conversational Spanish:

Se lo he dicho a Pedro. I have told Pedro.

VOCABULARY 4	
ofrecer	to offer
la taza	cup
enviar	to send
la carne	meat
el pescado	fish
comprender	to understand
vender	to sell
la bicicleta	bicycle

Exercise 5

Replace the words in brackets with the appropriate form of the object pronoun:

1 Juan ofrece (el pan) (a su amigo).
2 Bebo (una taza de té) por la mañana.
3 Hemos comprado (un coche).
4 Me ha enviado (unas flores).
5 He escrito (una carta) (a mi tía).
6 Comemos (la carne y el pescado).
7 Estos señores no comprenden (el inglés).
8 Tengo que estudiar (la lección).
9 Nos ha vendido (las bicicletas).
10 Hemos dado (los libros) (a Pedro).

5.9 THE IMPERATIVE: POLITE COMMANDS

In regular verbs, the polite imperative is formed by adding the following endings to the stem:

	singular	plural
	-e	**-en** to verbs ending in **-ar**
	-a	**-an** to verbs ending in **-er** and **-ir**

hablar	**hable (Vd.)**	**hablen (Vds.)** (Speak!)
comer	**coma (Vd.)**	**coman (Vds.)** (Eat!)
subir	**suba (Vd.)**	**suban (Vds.)** (Go up!)

Vd(s). can be added to make the request more polite.

Object pronouns are placed after the imperative, unless it is negative:

Bébalo (Vd.). Drink it.
No lo beba (Vd.). Don't drink it.
Envíeselo (Vd.). Send it to him.
No se lo envíe (Vd.). Don't send it to him.

In irregular verbs, the polite imperative is usually formed by adding the same endings as for regular verbs to the stem of the first-person singular of the present tense (not the stem of the infinitive):

	present	imperative
tener (to have)	**tengo**	**tenga Vd./tengan Vds.**
decir (to say)	**digo**	**diga Vd./digan Vds.**
contar (to count)	**cuento**	**cuente Vd./cuenten Vds.**

Note also the irregular forms of **ir**: **vaya Vd./vayan Vds.**

Exercise 6

Translate by using the singular polite imperative:

1 Don't smoke.
2 Drink this wine.
3 Send me the magazine.
4 Read them the letter.
5 Sell him your watch.
6 Learn these numbers.
7 Write your name here.
8 Don't eat those apples.
9 Don't buy that meat.
10 Don't give them to me.

Now, repeat the exercise, this time putting the imperative in the plural.

Drills 1–2

Example:
¿Has tomado el café? Did you have your coffee?
No, voy a tomarlo ahora. No, I'm going to have it now.

1 ¿Has tomado la cerveza?
2 ¿Han ido de compras?
3 ¿Ha escrito la carta?
4 ¿Habéis hecho el trabajo?
5 ¿Has comprado los libros?
6 ¿Han visto a su padre?
7 ¿Habéis terminado la comida?
8 ¿Ha llamado a Conchita?
9 ¿Ha subido (Vd.) las maletas?
10 ¿Habéis bebido el vino?

Example:
¿Preparo la comida? Shall I prepare the meal?
Sí, prepárela. Yes, prepare it.

¿Preparamos la comida? Shall we prepare the meal?
Sí, prepárenla. Yes, prepare it.

1 ¿Compro el periódico?
2 ¿Subimos las maletas?
3 ¿Llamo al profesor?
4 ¿Invitamos a esos amigos?
5 ¿Leo la carta?
6 ¿Enviamos estas flores?
7 ¿Me bebo esta cerveza?
8 ¿Vendemos esta bicicleta?

5

Drill 3

Example:
Beba (Vd.) el café.   Drink your coffee.
Ya lo he bebido.   I have already drunk it.

Beban (Vds.) el café.   Drink your coffee.
Ya lo hemos bebido.   We have already drunk it.

1 Prepare (Vd.) el pescado.
2 Llamen (Vds.) al perro.
3 Escriba (Vd.) su nombre.
4 Tomen (Vds.) la carne.
5 Compre (Vd.) los billetes.
6 Hablen (Vds.) a los profesores.
7 Cuente (Vd.) los libros.
8 Vendan (Vds.) el reloj.
9 Lea (Vd.) esta revista.

If you're interested in finding out how to form
the familiar imperative, go to section 11.6!

Un día muy ocupado

CARMEN ¿Qué vas a hacer hoy?

ANTONIO Hoy tengo varias cosas que hacer. Primero tengo que ir al banco, y después voy a ir a ver a Carlos, que está en el hospital.

CARMEN ¿En el hospital? ¿Qué le pasa?

ANTONIO Ha tenido un accidente de coche volviendo de Málaga.

CARMEN Y ¿ha sido muy grave?

ANTONIO No. Tiene una pierna rota y dos o tres heridas leves.

CARMEN ¡Pobre hombre! Tengo que llamar a su mujer y ofrecerle mi ayuda, si la necesita.

ANTONIO Sí, esa es una buena idea.

CARMEN Bueno, y, por la tarde, ¿qué vas a hacer?

ANTONIO Tengo que pasarme por la oficina, pero no voy a estar mucho tiempo.

CARMEN Entonces, ¿podemos ir al cine? Ponen una película francesa en el Roxy que deseo ver. Mi hermana la ha visto y me ha dicho que es muy buena.

ANTONIO Pues te espero a las siete menos cuarto en la puerta del cine. ¿Vale?

CARMEN Muy bien.

5

A very busy day

CARMEN What are you going to do today?

ANTONIO Today I have several things to do. First I have to go to the bank, and then I'm going to see Carlos, who is in the hospital.

CARMEN In the hospital? What happened to him?

ANTONIO He had a car accident coming back from Málaga.

CARMEN And was it very serious?

ANTONIO No. He has a broken leg and two or three minor injuries.

CARMEN Poor man! I must call his wife and offer my help if she needs it.

ANTONIO Yes, that's a good idea.

CARMEN Right, and in the afternoon, what are you going to do?

ANTONIO I have to go by the office, but I'm not going to be long.

CARMEN In that case, can we go to the movies? They're showing (lit. "They put") a French film at the Roxy that I want to see. My sister has seen it, and she told me that it's very good.

ANTONIO So ... I'll wait (lit. "I wait") for you at a quarter to seven outside the movie. All right?

CARMEN Fine.

Week 6

- *more question words and exclamations*
- *verbs that have a spelling change in the stem*
- *reflexive verbs (e.g., "to wash oneself")*
- *pronouns with prepositions*
- *some irregular verbs in the present tense*
- *idioms using* **hacer** *(to do, to make)*
- *impersonal verbs (used only in the "it" form)*
- *the verbs* **gustar** *(to like) and* **querer** *(to love, to want)*

6.1 SOME USEFUL QUESTION WORDS

¿Dónde? ¿Adónde?	Where? Where (to)?
¿Cómo?	How?
¿Cuándo?	When?
¿Cuánto/a/os/as?	How much? How many?
¿Por qué?	Why?

Note that **porque** written as one word means "because."
¿Verdad? (literally, "true") is used to seek corroboration
of a statement.

¿Dónde está la pluma?
Where is the pen?
¿Adónde vais?
Where are you going?
¿Cómo está (Vd.)?
How are you?
¿Cuándo salimos?
When are we going out?
¿Cuántos libros necesitas?
How many books do you need?
¿Por qué no compras el coche?
Why don't you buy the car?
Porque no tengo dinero.
Because I don't have any money.
Conchita es muy simpática, ¿verdad?
Conchita is very nice, isn't she?

6.2 EXCLAMATIONS

¡Cómo!	What! How …!
¡Cuánto/a/os/as!	How much …! What a lot …!
¡Qué!	What a …! How …!
¡Quién!	Would that I…/If only I …!
	(imperfect subjunctive)

¡Cómo pesa esta maleta!
How heavy this suitcase is!
¡Cómo! ¿No vas a venir a la fiesta?
What! You're not coming to the party?
¡Cuánto tenemos que hablar!
What a lot ("How much") we have to talk about!
¡Qué caras son estas manzanas!
How expensive these apples are!
¡Qué bonita iglesia!
What a lovely church!
¡Qué pena!
What a shame!
¡Qué amable!
How kind!
¡Qué asco!
How revolting!
¡Quién tuviera dinero!
If only I had money!

Note that if the noun that follows **¡Qué…!** is itself followed by an adjective, you need to insert either **tan** or **más** in front of the adjective:

¡Qué casa tan grande!
What a big house!
¡Qué mujer más trabajadora!
What a hard-working woman!
¡Qué niños tan traviesos!
How naughty the children are!

6.3 STEM-CHANGING VERBS

There are several Spanish verbs that have a spelling
change in the stem vowel when the stress falls on it: the
e may change to **ie,** the **o** to **ue,** and in some **-ir** verbs,
the **e** may change to **i.**

present tense

pensar	**volver**	**pedir**
to think	to return	to ask for
pienso	**vuelvo**	**pido**
piensas	**vuelves**	**pides**
piensa	**vuelve**	**pide**
pensamos	**volvemos**	**pedimos**
pensáis	**volvéis**	**pedís**
piensan	**vuelven**	**piden**

The first- and second-person plural remains regular, as the
stem vowel is not stressed. Verbs with a stem vowel
change will be shown in subsequent vocabulary lists thus:

pensar (ie); volver (ue); pedir (i)

6.4 REFLEXIVE VERBS (E.G., "I WASH MYSELF")

When the object of the verb is the same person or thing
as the subject, the verb is called reflexive. These are
much more common in Spanish than in English.

reflexive pronouns

me	myself
te	yourself
se	himself, herself, itself, yourself (pol.)
nos	ourselves
os	yourselves
se	themselves, yourselves (pol. pl.)

The third person of the reflexive pronoun, **se,** is attached
to the infinitive of reflexive verbs: e.g., **divertirse** (to
enjoy oneself).

6

lavarse	to wash oneself
sentarse (ie)	to sit down
dormirse (ue)	to fall asleep

Present tense of **lavarse**:
me lavo
te lavas
se lava
nos lavamos
os laváis
se lavan

Note that the reflexive pronoun cannot be omitted: it is part of the conjugation of the verb. Regarding their position, reflexive pronouns follow the same rules as object pronouns:

Me lavo. I wash myself.
Tengo que lavarme. I have to wash myself.
Estoy lavándome. I am washing myself.
Lávate. Wash yourself.
No te laves. Don't wash yourself.

Some verbs change their meaning when used reflexively:

llamar	to call
llamarse	to call oneself, to be called
ir	to go
irse	to go away
dormir	to sleep
dormirse	to go to sleep
llevar	to carry, to wear
llevarse	to take away

With some verbs, the reflexive pronoun may be used to give emphasis or finality to the action of the verb:

decidir, decidirse a	to decide
morir, morirse (ue)	to die
parar, pararse	to stop

6.5 RECIPROCAL FORM ("EACH OTHER")

The reflexive pronoun is also used in reciprocal verbs, such as:

quererse (ie)   to love each other
comprenderse   to understand each other
verse   to see each other

Mi hermano y yo no nos comprendemos.
My brother and I don't understand each other.

VOCABULARY 1

todos los días	every day
casarse	to get married
odiar(se)	to hate (each other)
ayudar(se)	to help (each other)
acostarse (ue)	to go to bed

6

Exercise 1

Translate:

1 Pedro and Anita write to each other every day.
2 The car is going to stop.
3 We are going to get married.
4 The children go to bed at eight o'clock.
5 We have to wash ourselves.
6 The two men hate each other.
7 He always asks me for money.
8 They never help each other.
9 Carlos returns from the office at half past six.
10 I must go to sleep.
11 Take away these cups!
12 The street is called Baeza.
13 I'm going to sit here.
14 We are going away tomorrow.
15 I have decided to live in Spain.

6.6 PERSONAL PRONOUNS WITH PREPOSITIONS

The pronouns used after prepositions, known as disjunctive or stressed pronouns, are the same as subject pronouns, except for **mí** (me), **ti** (you, familiar), and **sí** (himself, herself, yourself):

Estas cartas son para mí.
These letters are for me.
No vuelve con nosotros.
He's not coming back with us.
Vamos sin ella.
We're going without her.

With the preposition **con** (with), the forms **mí**, **ti**, and **sí** become **conmigo**, **contigo**, and **consigo**:

No puedo vivir contigo.
I can't live with you.
Siempre lleva un libro consigo.
He always carries a book with him(self).

Consigo can only be used reflexively; otherwise, the forms "with him," "with her," "with you," "with them" are translated by **con él**, **con ella**, **con Vd.**, etc.

VOCABULARY 2	
el regalo	present
para	for
el tiempo	weather (also, time)
contra	against
sin	without
siempre	always
el viaje	journey
entre	between
según	according to

Exercise 2

Translate:

1 We are working with them.
2 He has bought a present for me.
3 Is he going to come back with you (fam. sing.)?
4 The weather is against us.
5 They have gone away without him.
6 He has always lived with me.
7 These letters are for her.
8 They are going to buy the house between them.
9 Are the children with you (fam. sing.)?
10 According to him, the journey is too long.

6.7 IRREGULAR VERBS IN THE PRESENT TENSE

The following common verbs are irregular in the present tense, but only in the first-person singular:

poner (to put)	**pongo, pones, pone, ponemos, ponéis, ponen**
salir (to go out)	**salgo, sales, sale, salimos, salís, salen**
ver (to see)	**veo, ves, ve, vemos, veis, ven**
hacer (to do, to make)	**hago, haces, hace, hacemos, hacéis, hacen**
traer (to bring)	**traigo, traes, trae, traemos, traéis, traen**
dar (to give)	**doy, das, da, damos, dais, dan**
saber (to know)	**sé, sabes, sabe, sabemos, sabéis, saben**

6.8 IDIOMATIC USES OF **HACER**

Besides meaning "to do" and "to make," **hacer** is used:

1 in a number of impersonal expressions relating to the weather

¿Qué tiempo hace? What's the weather like?
Hace frío. It's cold.
Hace (mucho) calor. It's (very) hot.
Hace sol. It's sunny.
Hace viento. It's windy.
Hace buen día. It's a nice day.

2 in certain expressions of time

Hace muchos años ... Many years ago ...
Hace media hora ... Half an hour ago ...
¿Hace mucho tiempo que esperas?
Have you been waiting long?

3 in some other idiomatic expressions

hacer(se) daño	to hurt oneself
no hacer caso	to ignore, not to take any notice
hacerse rico	to become rich
hacer señas	to motion, to make a sign
hacerse a algo	to become used to something

6.9 IMPERSONAL VERBS

Impersonal verbs have a subject that is no person or entity in particular. They are used in the third-person singular, in the infinitive, or as a present participle.

llover (ue)	to rain
nevar (ie)	to snow
helar (ie)	to freeze
tronar (ue)	to thunder
amanecer	to dawn
anochecer	to get dark

6.10 THE VERB **GUSTAR** (TO LIKE)

The most natural-sounding equivalent of this verb in English is "to like," but its more direct translation is "to be pleasing to" or "to appeal to." This means that the verb conjugates according to the object being spoken about, and the person who likes it becomes an indirect object.

Me gusta el café. I like coffee. ("To me it is pleasing ...")
Nos gusta Inglaterra. We like England.
Te gustan las uvas. You like grapes.
A Carlos le gusta pintar. Carlos likes painting.

When the subject of **gustar** is an action, as in **pintar** (to paint) in the sentence above, this verb has to be in its infinitive form. Note also that the preposition **a** (to) must be used in front of the noun that is the indirect object.

Sometimes a disjunctive pronoun is used for emphasis or to indicate a contrast. For example:

¿A Vd. le gusta el flamenco? Do you like flamenco?
A mí no me gustan los deportes, pero a mi marido le gustan mucho.
I don't like sports, but my husband likes them very much.

There are several other Spanish verbs that have the same "inverse" construction as **gustar**:

bastar (to suffice, to be enough)
Este dinero me basta. This money is enough for me.

faltar (to be missing, to be short of)
Siempre les falta tiempo. They are always short of time.

hacer falta (to need, to be necessary)
Nos hace falta más vino. We need more wine.

parecer (to seem, to think of)
¿Qué te parecen estos pantalones?
What do you think of these pants?

6

quedar (to remain, to have left)
¿Le quedan entradas para la función de la tarde?
Do you have any tickets left for the evening performance?

sobrar (to be/have more than enough)
Nos sobra tiempo para llegar a la estación.
We have more than enough time to get to the station.

Exercise 3

Translate:

1 What's the weather like?
2 Today it's very cold.
3 It's going to rain tomorrow.
4 I don't like this beer.
5 He is going to bring us coffee.
6 He likes to go out every evening.
7 I don't know where it is.
8 They go to Spain because they like the sun.
9 Twenty-five years ago
10 Carmen likes to sit in the garden.

6.11 THE VERB QUERER (IE)

This verb means "to want" and "to wish" and is also used to express love for a person. It is not used in the sense of "to like" (see **gustar** in the previous section), although "I'd like" is translated by **quisiera** (imperfect subjunctive).

Quiero a mis hijos. I love my children.
No quieren ir a Francia. They don't want to go to France.
Quisiera ver a Ramón. I'd like to see Ramon.

Drills 1–2

Example:
¿Os gusta a vosotros España? Do you like Spain?
Sí, nos gusta mucho. Yes, we like it very much.

1 ¿Te gusta a ti la playa?
2 ¿Le gustan a Carlos los deportes?
3 ¿Os gusta a vosotros vivir en Madrid?
4 ¿Os gusta la cerveza?
5 ¿Le gusta a Conchita el regalo?
6 ¿Te gustan los niños?
7 ¿Os gusta a vosotros viajar?
8 ¿Les gusta a tus amigos el vino?
9 ¿Les gusta a Vds. el hotel?
10 ¿Les gusta a ellos el pescado?

Example:
(Vosotros) vais con Carlos, ¿verdad? You're going with Carlos, aren't you?
Sí, vamos con él. Yes, we're going with him.

1 Trabaja (Vd.) con María, ¿verdad?
2 Esta carta es para nosotros, ¿verdad?
3 Su hermano vuelve contigo, ¿verdad?
4 Vamos al teatro sin los niños, ¿verdad?
5 Estas flores son para mí, ¿verdad?
6 Vive con sus padres, ¿verdad?
7 Estos periódicos son para Vds., ¿verdad?
8 Vas de compras con tu marido, ¿verdad?

6

Drill 3

Example:

¿Quieres acostarte? Do you want to go to bed?
Sí, quisiera acostarme. Yes, I'd like to go to bed.

¿Queréis acostaros? Do you want to go to bed?
Sí, quisiéramos acostarnos. Yes, we'd like to go to bed.

1 ¿Quiere Vd. sentarse?
2 ¿Quieres lavarte?
3 ¿Quieres dormirte?
4 ¿Quieres irte?
5 ¿Quiere Vd. pararse?

6 ¿Quieren Vds. sentarse?
7 ¿Queréis lavaros?
8 ¿Queréis dormiros?
9 ¿Queréis iros?
10 ¿Quieren Vds. pararse?

6

CONVERSATION

Planes de vacaciones

MIGUEL **¿Adónde vais de vacaciones este año?**

PILAR **Vamos a un pueblo de la costa del Mediterráneo, cerca de Valencia.**

MIGUEL **¿En qué mes vais?**

PILAR **Vamos en julio porque hace muy buen tiempo. Hace calor y el mar está estupendo para bañarse.**

MIGUEL **A nosotros nos gusta más el norte. Todos los años vamos a Santander en agosto.**

PILAR **Pero en el norte hace mal tiempo, llueve mucho y hay muchos días en los que es imposible ir a la playa.**

MIGUEL **Es verdad. Pero no vamos buscando el sol, vamos huyendo del calor de Madrid, que en agosto es insoportable.**

PILAR **Pues a mí me gusta el calor. Ya tenemos bastante frío todo el invierno.**

MIGUEL **Yo, sin embargo, prefiero el invierno al verano.**

PILAR **¡Sobre gustos no hay nada escrito!**

Vacation plans

MIGUEL Where are you going on vacation this year?

PILAR We're going to a village on the Mediterranean coast, near Valencia.

MIGUEL Which month are you going?

PILAR We're going in July because the weather is very good. It's warm and the sea is lovely to bathe in.

MIGUEL We like the north better. Every year we go to Santander in August.

PILAR But in the north the weather is bad, it rains a lot, and there are many days when it's impossible to go to the beach.

MIGUEL That's true. But we're not going for (lit. "seeking") the sun, we're trying to get away (lit. "we go fleeing") from the heat in Madrid, which in August is unbearable.

PILAR Well, I like the heat. We are cold enough all through the winter.

MIGUEL I, on the other hand, prefer winter to summer.

PILAR There's no accounting for tastes!

Week 7

- the imperfect tense ("I was doing," "I used to do")
- the verb **soler**
- the past perfect ("I had done")
- more negative words (never, nothing, neither, etc.)
- adverbs ("easily," "frequently," etc.)
- comparison of adjectives, adverbs, and nouns (more ... than, less ... than, as ... as)

7.1 THE IMPERFECT TENSE ("WAS DOING," "USED TO DO")

In Spanish, the imperfect is a simple (single word) tense used to indicate a regular, repeated action or a continuous description of an action that occurred over an indefinite period of time. In English, this is usually rendered by "was/were" + present participle or "used to" + infinitive.

Here is the regular conjugation of the imperfect tense for **-ar, -er,** and **-ir** verbs:

hablar	comer	vivir
to speak	to eat	to live
hablaba	comía	vivía
hablabas	comías	vivías
hablaba	comía	vivía
hablábamos	comíamos	vivíamos
hablabais	comíais	vivíais
hablaban	comían	vivían

Carlos compraba el periódico todos los días.
Carlos used to buy the newspaper every day.
El hombre vendía caramelos.
The man was selling sweets.

As the first- and third-person singular have the same forms, the subject pronoun is sometimes used to avoid ambiguity.

There are only three verbs that are irregular in the imperfect tense: **ser, ir,** and **ver**.

<u>ser</u>	<u>ir</u>	<u>ver</u>
to be	to go	to see
era	**iba**	**veía**
eras	**ibas**	**veías**
era	**iba**	**veía**
éramos	**íbamos**	**veíamos**
erais	**ibais**	**veíais**
eran	**iban**	**veían**

Íbamos a España una vez al año.
We used to go to Spain once a year.

"There was" and "there were" are translated by **había** (the imperfect of the verb **haber**):

Había mucha gente en la playa.
There were a lot of people on the beach.
Había un atasco en la plaza.
There was a traffic jam in the square.

7

7.2 THE VERB SOLER (UE)

This verb is used only in the present and imperfect. It conveys "to be used to" or "to usually do something" and is found in contexts that are expressed in English with "generally," "usually," or "as a rule":

Suelo levantarme a las siete.
I usually get up at seven.
Solíamos ir de paseo los domingos.
We used to go for a walk on Sundays.

7.3 THE PAST PERFECT (E.G., "HAD DONE")

This is a compound tense formed with the imperfect of the auxiliary verb **haber** and the past participle of the main verb. For example:

Habíamos comido. We had eaten.
Habían escrito. They had written.
Ramón había salido. Ramon had gone out.

VOCABULARY 1

el/la gerente	manager
los bombones	chocolates
el/la muchacho/a	boy/girl
buscar	to look for
la función	performance
empezar (ie)	to begin
la fábrica	factory
el mar	sea
mirar	to look at

Exercise 1

Translate:

1 Luis was selling a car.
2 I usually see her in the morning.
3 They had spoken to the hotel manager.
4 He used to bring me chocolates.
5 The boy was looking for his suitcase.
6 The performance used to start at ten o'clock.
7 He had worked in a factory.
8 The sea was very cold.
9 The woman was looking at us.
10 We usually ate a lot of fish.

SOME NEGATIVE WORDS: NEVER, NOTHING, NEITHER, ETC.

jamás, nunca	never
nada	nothing
tampoco	neither
nadie	no one, nobody
ninguno/a	none
ni ... ni	neither ... nor

Nunca sale de casa.
He never goes out of the house.
Nadie lo había visto.
Nobody had seen it.
Ni fuma ni bebe.
He neither smokes nor drinks.

Note that in Spanish, the double negative is not incorrect and occurs frequently:

No necesito nada.
I don't need anything.
Mi padre no lo sabe tampoco.
My father doesn't know either.
No escribe nunca.
He never writes.

Ninguno/a can play the role of an adjective or pronoun. It may refer to people or things, and it is always used in the singular. As an adjective, the masculine form is shortened to **ningún** in front of the noun:

No hay ningún niño en la playa.
There aren't any children on the beach.
Voy a comprar sellos, no tengo ninguno.
I'm going to buy stamps, I don't have any.

See the next page for the affirmative forms that correspond to these negatives, e.g., always, some, something, someone.

7

siempre	always
algo	something
también	also, too
alguien	someone, somebody
alguno/a	some, any
o … o	either … or

Alguien ha preguntado por Vd.
Someone has asked for you.
O canta, o baila.
Either he sings, or he dances.

Like its opposite **ninguno** (none), **alguno** (some) is shortened to **algún** in front of a masculine noun. It is sometimes used in the singular when a plural form would be typical in English.

Quiero comprar algún periódico.
I want to buy some newspapers.

VOCABULARY 2

conocer	to know, to be familiar with, to meet
la leche	milk
venir (ie)	to come
poder	to be able to
ocurrir	to happen

Exercise 2

Fill in the blanks with the appropriate negative word:

1 Juan no quiere hacer ....
2 No conocemos a ... en esta ciudad.
3 No tienen ... pan ... leche.
4 María no viene ... a verme.
5 No he leído ... libro de Cervantes.
6 Carlos no puede ir y su hermano ....
7 ... sabe lo que ha ocurrido.
8 No hay ... nuevo.
9 No hemos comprado ... revista.
10 Esa mujer no ha trabajado ....

7.5 ADVERBS (E.G., "EASILY," "FREQUENTLY")

Many adverbs are formed in Spanish by adding the ending **-mente** to the feminine form of the adjective:

maravillosamente wonderfully
fácilmente easily
frecuentemente frequently

When two or more adverbs ending in **-mente** follow one another, only the last one ends in **-mente**; the others keep the feminine form of the adjective:

El niño ha sido castigado justa y severamente.
The boy has been punished justly and severely.

When using some adverbs, there is an occasional pitfall or special construction to watch out for. Here are some examples.

1 ahora now

¿Qué vas a hacer ahora?
What are you going to do now?

2 ya now, already, (no) longer, yet (in a question)

Ya lo veo.
I can see now.
Ya han terminado de comer.
They have already finished eating.
Ya no vivimos en esa casa.
We no longer live in that house.
¿Se ha despertado ya?
Has he woken up yet?

Note that **ya** is often used simply for emphasis; in this case, it is not translated in English:

¡Ya lo verás! You'll see!
¡Ya voy! I'm coming!
¡Ya lo creo! I should think so!

3 entonces then (at that time, in that case)

Yo trabajaba entonces en una compañía de seguros.
I was then working for an insurance company.
¿No quieres venir al cine? Entonces iré yo solo.
Don't you want to come to the movies? Then I'll go
alone/by myself.

4 luego then (next, soon after, later)

**Primero tenemos que ir al banco y luego al
mercado.**
First we have to go to the bank and then to the market.
¡Hasta luego!
See you later!
Desde luego.
Of course.

Exercise 3

Form adverbs from the following adjectives:

1 feliz (happy)
2 verdadero (true)
3 triste (sad)
4 lento (slow)
5 nuevo (new)
6 agradable (pleasant)
7 malo (bad)
8 cierto (certain)
9 rápido (fast)
10 claro (clear)

7.6 COMPARISON OF ADJECTIVES AND ADVERBS

The comparison of equality "as ... as" is rendered by
tan ... como:

Carlos es tan alto como Pedro.
Carlos is as tall as Pedro.
Nadie habla tan despacio como Juan.
Nobody talks as slowly as Juan.

The comparison of inequality (more ... than, less ... than)
is rendered by **más ... que, menos ... que**:

Yo soy más pobre que Vd.
I am poorer than you.
María es menos inteligente que su hermana.
Maria is less intelligent than her sister.
Mi mujer ha llegado más tarde que yo.
My wife arrived later than I did.
Este hombre trabaja menos diligentemente que aquel.
This man works less diligently than that one.

7

7.7 IRREGULAR COMPARATIVES: ADJECTIVES

bueno (good)→ **mejor** (better)
malo (bad)→ **peor** (worse)
mucho (a lot of)→ **más** (more)
poco (little, few)→ **menos** (less, fewer)
grande (big)→ **mayor** (bigger, older)
pequeño (small)→ **menor** (smaller, younger)

Grande and **pequeño** also have a regular comparative,
más grande and **más pequeño**, which refers only to size:

Esta casa es más grande que la mía.
This house is bigger than mine.

Mejor, **peor**, **mayor**, and **menor** have a plural form
ending in **-es**: the same form is used for both genders.

7.8 IRREGULAR COMPARATIVES: ADVERBS

bien (well)→ **mejor** (better)
mal (badly)→ **peor** (worse)
mucho (much)→ **más** (more)
poco (little)→ **menos** (less)

Pilar canta mal, pero yo canto peor que ella.
Pilar sings badly, but I sing worse than she does.

7.9 COMPARISON OF NOUNS

The comparison of inequality is constructed in the same way for nouns as for adjectives and adverbs: **más … que, menos … que**:

Carmen tiene más paciencia que Pilar.
Carmen has more patience than Pilar.
Tengo menos libros que tú.
I have fewer books than you.

The comparison of equality is expressed by **tanto … como**. As **tanto** is an adjective, it has to agree in gender and number with the following noun:

No he bebido tanto zumo como Pedro.
I haven't drunk as much juice as Pedro.
Vd. no recibe tantas cartas como yo.
You don't receive as many letters as I do.

VOCABULARY 3

fuerte	strong
el jerez	sherry
seco	dry
negro	black
el zapato	shoe
azul	blue
pronto	soon
necesitar	to need
el agua (f.)	water
caliente	hot, warm
la piscina	swimming pool
el zumo	juice

7

Exercise 4

Translate:

1 My brother is stronger than I (am).
2 This sherry is drier than that one.
3 Carlos is three years older than Maria.
4 The black shoes are smaller than the blue (ones).
5 His car is better than mine.
6 He writes worse than his sister.
7 I have arrived sooner than my father.
8 They don't have as much money as their friends.
9 I don't need as many suitcases as you (fam. sing.).
10 The water in the pool is warmer than in the sea.

Drill 1

Example:
¿Ibais al mercado? Did you use to go to the market?
Sí, solíamos ir. Yes, we used to go.

¿Leías el periódico? Did you use to read the paper?
Sí, solía leerlo. Yes, I used to read it.

1 ¿Veías a Carmen?
2 ¿Comían en el hotel?
3 ¿Trabajaban (Vds.)?
4 ¿Escribías cartas?
5 ¿Viajaba a Londres?
6 ¿Ibais al café?
7 ¿Hablaba (Vd.) español?
8 ¿Invitaba a sus amigos?
9 ¿Tenían dinero?
10 ¿Bebías zumo?

Drills 2–3

Example:
¿Ha venido alguien? Has anyone come?
No, no ha venido nadie. No, no one has come.

1 ¿Quiere (Vd.) algo?

2 ¿Han vivido aquí siempre?

3 ¿Quieren (Vds.) té o café?

4 ¿Hay algún turista inglés?

5 ¿Conocen (Vds.) a alguien?

6 ¿Tiene (Vd.) alguna revista española?

Example:
Mi casa es pequeña. My house is small.
La mía es más pequeña. Mine is smaller.

1 Mis libros son viejos.

2 Mi coche es malo.

3 Mi jardín es bonito.

4 Mi hotel es bueno.

5 Mi marido es alto.

6 Mis zapatos son caros.

7 Mis maletas son grandes.

8 Mis pantalones son baratos.

7

CONVERSATION

El Sr. Sánchez habla con su secretaria.

SR. SÁNCHEZ **Buenos días, Lucía. Llego más tarde que de costumbre.**

LUCÍA **Sí. ¿Qué le ha ocurrido? Son casi las diez.**

SR. SÁNCHEZ **El coche no arrancaba esta mañana. Como ha helado durante la noche, el motor estaba muy frío.**

LUCÍA **¡Qué lata! Por eso yo nunca vengo en el coche. Uso el metro. Es mucho más rápido y me ahorro muchos problemas.**

SR. SÁNCHEZ **Claro. Así no tiene gastos ni de gasolina ni de aparcamiento. Yo creo que voy a hacer lo mismo pronto.**

LUCÍA **Es lo mejor. No lo dude.**

SR. SÁNCHEZ **¿Ha venido alguien?**

LUCÍA **No. No ha venido nadie.**

SR. SÁNCHEZ **Y, ¿hay algún recado?**

LUCÍA **No, nada. Hay algunas cartas que he dejado en su escritorio.**

SR. SÁNCHEZ **Bueno. Entonces, voy a ver el correo, y dentro de media hora venga a mi despacho porque quiero organizar una reunión con nuestros clientes.**

LUCÍA **Muy bien, Sr. Sánchez.**

Mr. Sánchez speaks with his personal assistant.

MR. SÁNCHEZ Good morning, Lucía. I'm (lit. "I arrive") later than usual.

LUCÍA Yes. What happened to you? It's almost ten o'clock.

MR. SÁNCHEZ The car wouldn't start (lit. "was not starting") this morning. As it froze (lit. "has frozen") during the night, the engine was very cold.

LUCÍA What a pain! That's why I never come in the car. I use the metro. It's much quicker, and I save myself all the hassle.

MR. SÁNCHEZ Of course. That way you don't have any gas or parking expenses. I think I'm going to do the same soon.

LUCÍA It's the best thing. Believe me. (lit. "Don't doubt it.")

MR. SÁNCHEZ Has anyone come by?

LUCÍA No. No one has come.

MR. SÁNCHEZ And are there any messages?

LUCÍA No, nothing. There are some letters that I've left on your desk.

MR. SÁNCHEZ All right. I'm going to check the mail then; and in half an hour come to my office, because I want to organize a meeting with our clients.

LUCÍA Fine, Mr. Sánchez.

7

Review exercises

Drill 1

Work through this drill in exactly the same way as all the others you've done so far.

¿Qué prefieres, el té o el café?
What do you prefer, tea or coffee?

Me gusta más el café.
I like coffee better./I prefer coffee.

1 ¿Qué prefieren (ustedes), el vino o la cerveza?
... el vino.

2 ¿Qué preferís, la carne o el pescado?
... la carne.

3 ¿Qué prefiere Sofía, el campo o la playa?
... la playa.

4 ¿Qué prefieres, el fútbol o el rugby?
... el rugby.

5 ¿Qué prefieren los niños, jugar o ver la televisión?
... jugar.

6 ¿Qué prefiere usted, Barcelona o Madrid?
... Barcelona.

Exercise 1

Translate:

1 I'm going to a party tomorrow, and I need a new dress.

2 We have seen a very good film at the Roxy.

3 He can't come to the beach with us, he's got too much work.

4 Pedro is very pleasant, but he has no patience with the children.

5 The performance doesn't start until 10:15 p.m.—it's too late for us.

6 They haven't been able to go out because it has rained all day.

7 We have to wait until 4:30 p.m. because the shops are closed (cerradas).

Drill 2

Practice your polite imperatives!

¿Compro el pan? Shall I buy the bread?

Sí, cómprelo. Yes, buy it.
No, no lo compre. No, don't buy it.

1 ¿Lavo este vestido?
Sí, ...

2 ¿Espero a Carmen?
No, ...

3 ¿Pregunto a ese señor?
Sí, ...

4 ¿Me llevo las tazas?
No, ...

5 ¿Llamo al gerente?
Sí, ...

6 ¿Invito a Miguel?
No, ...

7 ¿Pongo las flores en agua?
Sí, ...

8 ¿Hago el café?
No, ...

When you've done this drill, answering "Sí" or "No" as indicated, you could work through it again and reverse your replies ... you won't find these alternatives in the answer key, but it's useful extra practice. And if you want some more extra practice, go to section 11.6 to find out about the familiar imperative and try forming the commands for an informal context.

Drill 3

More imperatives!

¿Compramos el pan? Shall we buy the bread?

Sí, cómprenlo. Yes, buy it.
No, no lo compren. No, don't buy it.

1 ¿Terminamos el vino?
Sí, ….

2 ¿Pedimos el pescado?
No, ….

3 ¿Vemos la habitación?
Sí, ….

4 ¿Nos bañamos en la piscina?
No, ….

5 ¿Compramos unos periódicos?
Sí, ….

6 ¿Preparamos la cena?
No, ….

7 ¿Enviamos las cartas?
Sí, ….

8 ¿Ayudamos a Pedro?
Sí, ….

Exercise 2

Complete the sentences given in column A with the correct sentence from column B:

A   B

1 Juan está en el hospital …   **a)** el agua estaba fría.

2 Queremos ir al cine …   **b)** hay demasiados turistas.

3 Vienen todos los años a España …   **c)** ha ido a llamar por teléfono.

4 El viernes es su cumpleaños …   **d)** se ha roto una pierna.

5 Estoy esperando a mi marido…   **e)** si queremos comprar todos esos regalos.

6 No han querido bañarse en la piscina …   **f)** les gusta mucho el sol.

7 Vamos a necesitar más dinero …   **g)** ponen una película muy buena.

8 No me gustan los pueblos de la costa …   **h)** va a dar una fiesta en su casa.

Exercise 3

Here is a conversation between you and Maria about your friend Luisa's birthday. Put your words into Spanish.

USTED   The day after tomorrow is Luisa's birthday.

MARÍA   Sí, tenemos que comprarle un regalo.

USTED   What can we buy her?

MARÍA   No sé, ¿tienes alguna idea?

USTED   I can only think of chocolates, flowers …

MARÍA   No, no. Tiene que ser algo más original.

USTED   She reads a lot, and she likes to travel. Why don't we buy her a travel book (libro de viajes)?

MARÍA   Bueno, eso es una posibilidad.

USTED   Then let's go shopping this afternoon, and we'll look ("we look") for something.

MARÍA   ¡Vale!

Week 8

- *shortened forms of adjectives*
- *adjectives that always precede the noun*
- *three frequent verbs that are irregular in the present tense and some irregular past participles*
- *the future tense (e.g., "will do")*
- *the conditional (e.g., "would do")*
- *verbs preceded by prepositions*
- *idioms using* **llevar** *(to wear, to carry) and* **hacer** *(to do, to make)*

8.1 SHORTENED ADJECTIVES

The following adjectives have shortened forms:

1 only before a masculine noun (before a feminine noun, the feminine must be used)

bueno (good)	**buen**
malo (bad)	**mal**
alguno (some)	**algún**
ninguno (none)	**ningún**
primero (first)	**primer**
tercero (third)	**tercer**
uno (one)	**un**

2 before nouns of either gender

grande (big)	**gran**
ciento (100)	**cien**
cualquiera (any)	**cualquier**

un buen libro   a good book
una buena película   a good film
el primer tren   the first train
la primera fila   the first row
cualquier autobús   any bus
cualquier persona   any person

8.2 ADJECTIVES THAT PRECEDE THE NOUN

Adjectives in Spanish usually follow the noun, but there are exceptions. Those that precede the noun include:

1 adjectives of quantity

mucho	a lot of
poco	little
tanto	so much
cuanto	how much
demasiado	too much
bastante	enough

2 indefinite adjectives

alguno	some, any
ninguno	none
cada	each
otro	other
todo	all
tal	such

cada is an invariable word:

cada hombre y cada mujer
each man and each woman

otro is never preceded by the indefinite article:

otro hombre y otra mujer
another man and another woman

tal is invariable and never followed by the indefinite article (though it can precede **tal** in specific cases: **ha llamado un tal Antonio** a certain Antonio called):

tal hombre y tal mujer
such a man and such a woman

3 numbers – but see section 4.4 for exceptions.

8

4 Some common adjectives, such as **bueno** (good), **malo** (bad), **pequeño** (small), **hermoso** (beautiful), **joven** (young), and **viejo** (old) often precede the noun:

un hermoso paisaje a beautiful landscape
un joven guitarrista a young guitarist

Certain adjectives change meaning when placed before or after the noun:

grande
una casa grande a big house
but
una gran mujer a great (famous) woman

nuevo
un coche nuevo a (brand) new car
but
un nuevo coche a new (different) car

pobre
un hombre pobre a poor (impecunious) man
but
un pobre hombre an unfortunate man

mismo
el mismo hombre the same man
but
el hombre mismo the man himself

While these are the basic rules, the position of adjectives in Spanish is fairly flexible and is often determined by a choice of emphasis, balance, and style; observation and practice will help you pick up the right usage.

8

el pintor/la pintora	painter
llevar	to wear, to carry
la ropa	clothes
la zona	area
perder (ie)	to lose
el bolso	handbag
el sombrero	hat
la bebida	drink
el sello	postage stamp
el nadador/	swimmer
la nadadora	

Exercise 1

Translate:

1 We have had a good journey.
2 Each man had a job.
3 She is a great painter.
4 They always wear the same clothes.
5 There are enough hotels in this area.
6 The poor woman has lost her handbag.
7 I have a brand-new hat.
8 We have asked for another drink.
9 These stamps are very old.
10 All the children are good swimmers.

8

8.3 THREE IRREGULAR VERBS (PRESENT TENSE)

venir	**oír**	**decir**
to come	to hear	to say, to tell
vengo	**oigo**	**digo**
vienes	**oyes**	**dices**
viene	**oye**	**dice**
venimos	**oímos**	**decimos**
venís	**oís**	**decís**
vienen	**oyen**	**dicen**

8.4 SOME IRREGULAR PAST PARTICIPLES

abrir (to open)→ **abierto** (opened)
morir (to die)→ **muerto** (died)
poner (to put)→ **puesto** (put)
romper (to break)→ **roto** (broken)
volver (to return)→ **vuelto** (returned)
describir (to describe)→ **descrito** (described)

(See section 5.2 for some others.)

8.5 THE FUTURE TENSE (E.G., "WILL DO")

The future tense of regular verbs is formed by adding
the following endings to the infinitive: **-é**, **-ás**, **-á**,
-emos, **-éis**, **-án**.

hablar	comer	vivir
to speak	to eat	to live

hablar	comer	vivir
hablaré	**comeré**	**viviré**
hablarás	**comerás**	**vivirás**
hablará	**comerá**	**vivirá**
hablaremos	**comeremos**	**viviremos**
hablaréis	**comeréis**	**viviréis**
hablarán	**comerán**	**vivirán**

Hablaremos en español todo el tiempo.
We will speak Spanish all the time.
Comerá con nosotros mañana.
He will eat with us tomorrow.
Vivirán cerca de sus padres.
They will live near his parents.

8.6 IRREGULAR VERBS IN THE FUTURE TENSE

A few verbs are irregular in the future tense. The endings remain the same as for regular verbs, but the stem changes:

caber (to fit in)	**cabré, cabrás,** etc.
decir (to say)	**diré, dirás,** etc.
haber (to have [aux.])	**habré, habrás,** etc.
hacer (to do)	**haré, harás,** etc.
poder (to be able to)	**podré, podrás,** etc.
poner (to put)	**pondré, pondrás,** etc.
querer (to want)	**querré, querrás,** etc.
saber (to know)	**sabré, sabrás,** etc.
salir (to go out)	**saldré, saldrás,** etc.
tener (to have)	**tendré, tendrás,** etc.
valer (to be worth)	**valdré, valdrás,** etc.
venir (to come)	**vendré, vendrás,** etc.

No podremos ir. We won't be able to go.
Diré unas pocas palabras. I'll say a few words.
Vendrán con él. They will come with him.

8.7 THE CONDITIONAL (E.G., "WOULD DO")

8

The conditional is formed by adding the following endings to the infinitive: **-ía, -ías, -ía, -íamos, -íais, -ían.**

hablar	comer	vivir
hablaría	**comería**	**viviría**
hablarías	**comerías**	**vivirías**
hablaría	**comería**	**viviría**
hablaríamos	**comeríamos**	**viviríamos**
hablaríais	**comeríais**	**viviríais**
hablarían	**comerían**	**vivirían**

As the first- and third-person singular have the same forms, the subject pronoun is sometimes used in order to avoid ambiguity: **yo viviría ...** I would live ...

Me gustaría ir a la fiesta.
I would like to go to the party.
No vivirían en España.
They would not live in Spain.

8.8 IRREGULAR VERBS IN THE CONDITIONAL

Verbs that are irregular in the future tense are also irregular in the conditional, with the same stem change:

decir→ diría; hacer→ haría; tener→ tendría; venir→ vendría, etc.

Yo quería saber lo que diría.
I wanted to know what he would say.
Tendrían que pagar el daño.
They would have to pay for the damage.

8.9 USES OF THE FUTURE AND CONDITIONAL

There are substantial differences between the use of the future and conditional in English and in Spanish. In Spanish, they can be used to express probability or assumption:

¿Por qué no ha venido Pedro?
Why hasn't Pedro come?
Estará enfermo.
He is probably ill.
¿Cuántos años tenía el niño?
How old was the boy?
Tendría nueve años.
He must have been nine.

The English "will" and "would" expressing will or determination are translated by **querer**:

No quiere contestar el teléfono.
He will not answer the phone.

No quería venir con nosotros.
He would not come with us.
¿Quiere (Vd.) un café?
Will you have a coffee?
¿Quiere (Vd.) cerrar la puerta, por favor?
Will you shut the door, please?

"Shall" introducing a suggestion, as in the following examples, is translated by the present tense:

¿Nos sentamos?
Shall we sit down?
¿Llamo a la policía?
Shall I call the police?

"Should" introducing an obligation or recommendation is translated by the conditional form of **deber**:

Deberías decirles la verdad.
You should tell them the truth.
Miguel debería dejar de fumar.
Miguel should give up smoking.

VOCABULARY 2

próximo	next
temprano	early
esta noche	tonight
conducir	to drive
andar	to walk
lejos	far
el museo	museum
el autocar	coach

Exercise 2

Translate:

1 They will get married next month.
2 I will go to bed early tonight.
3 He will come with us on vacation.
4 We will visit them on Sunday.
5 They will not speak to us.
6 It would be better to stop.
7 I wouldn't like to drive a big car.
8 He won't have to walk very far.
9 They wouldn't be worth anything.
10 We won't be able to see the museum.
11 He would not sell the house.
12 The coach will leave at eight o'clock.

8.10 VERBS WITH PREPOSITIONS

A verb that is preceded by a preposition must always be an infinitive:

Lo veré antes de salir.
I'll see him before leaving.
Se ha ido sin hablar con nosotros.
He left without speaking to us.

VOCABULARY 3

cerrar (ie)	to close
la ventana	window
antes de	before
después de	after
de	of, from
pasar	to spend (time)
llorar	to cry
sentirse (ie)	to feel
enfermo	ill
el marisco	seafood
la habitación	room
tomar	to take
la voz	voice
ronco	hoarse
gritar	to shout
enseñar	to show

Exercise 3

Translate:

1 I'll close the windows before going to bed.
2 I'll have to think before deciding.
3 You (fam. sing.) can't go without finishing the job.
4 He has spent the day without speaking to anyone.
5 She was crying without knowing why.
6 They were feeling ill after eating seafood.
7 I was very sleepy after working all night.
8 We would like to see the room before taking it.
9 His voice was hoarse from shouting so much.
10 After writing the letter, show it to me (pol.).

8.11 IDIOMATIC USES OF **LLEVAR** AND **HACER**

The verbs **llevar** (to wear, to carry) and **hacer** (to do, to make) are often used to express how long an action has or had been going on:

¿Cuánto tiempo llevas en España?
How long have you been in Spain?
Hace tres meses que estoy aquí.
I have been here three months.
¿Cuánto tiempo lleváis esperando?
How long have you been waiting?
Hace media hora que esperamos.
We've been waiting half an hour.

The question and answer can be reversed thus:

¿Cuánto tiempo hace que está (Vd.) en España?
Llevo tres meses aquí.

¿Cuánto tiempo hace que esperan (Vds.)?
Llevamos media hora esperando.

Drills 1–2

Example:
¿Ha venido tu amigo? Has your friend come?
No, vendrá luego. No, he will come later.

¿Ha leído (Vd.) el periódico? Have you read the newspaper?
No, lo leeré luego. No, I'll read it later.

1 ¿Han visto a su padre?
2 ¿Han terminado (Vds.) el trabajo?
3 ¿Has ido al banco?
4 ¿Ha escrito Pedro la carta?
5 ¿Habéis enviado las flores?
6 ¿Han cerrado la tienda?
7 ¿Ha salido Juan?
8 ¿Has hecho la comida?
9 ¿Han visto las habitaciones?
10 ¿Has abierto las ventanas?

Study the examples in section 8.11 and then do the following drill:

1 ¿Cuánto tiempo llevas estudiando español?
   … seis meses ….
2 ¿Cuánto tiempo lleváis en Madrid?
   … tres años ….
3 ¿Cuánto tiempo llevan ellos trabajando aquí?
   … dos semanas ….
4 ¿Cuánto tiempo lleva Juan viviendo en Los Ángeles?
   … un año ….
5 ¿Cuánto tiempo llevas esperando?
   … diez minutos ….
6 ¿Cuánto tiempo hace que estudias español?
   … seis meses ….
7 ¿Cuánto tiempo hace que estáis en Madrid?
   … tres años ….
8 ¿Cuánto tiempo hace que ellos trabajan aquí?
   … dos semanas ….
9 ¿Cuánto tiempo hace que Juan vive en Los Ángeles?
   … un año ….
10 ¿Cuánto tiempo hace que espera (Vd.)?
   … diez minutos ….

8

Un encuentro en la calle

PEDRO   **Teresa, ¡cuánto tiempo sin vernos!**

TERESA   **¿Cómo estás?**

PEDRO   **Muy bien, gracias. Y tú ¿qué haces en Madrid? ¿No vivías en Sevilla?**

TERESA   **Ya no. Mi marido está trabajando aquí ahora. Llevamos tres meses en Madrid.**

PEDRO   **¡Ah, muy bien! ¿Habéis encontrado piso ya?**

TERESA   **No. De momento estamos viviendo con los padres de Antonio. Pero el piso no es muy grande y estamos un poco apretados.**

PEDRO   **¿Qué tipo de piso buscáis? Porque tengo un amigo que vende uno con tres dormitorios, salón, comedor, cocina y baño. Y también tiene una terraza bastante grande. Lo que no sé es lo que pide. ¿Crees que puede interesarte?**

TERESA   **¡Ya lo creo! Si el precio es razonable. ¿Cómo podemos ponernos en contacto con él?**

PEDRO   **Se llama Alberto Solís, y estos son su teléfono y sus señas.**

TERESA   **Pues muchísimas gracias, Pedro. A ver si tenemos suerte.**

PEDRO   **Eso espero. Hasta pronto.**

TERESA   **Sí. Te llamaremos. Adiós.**

A chance meeting in the street

PEDRO Teresa, we haven't seen each other for a long time!

TERESA How are you?

PEDRO Very well, thanks. And you, what are you doing in Madrid? Weren't you living in Seville?

TERESA Not anymore. My husband is working here now. We have been in Madrid three months.

PEDRO Oh, great! Have you found an apartment yet?

TERESA No. At the moment we're living with Antonio's parents. But the apartment isn't very big, and we're a little cramped.

PEDRO What sort of apartment are you looking for? Because I have a friend who is selling one with three bedrooms, a living room, dining room, kitchen, and bathroom. It also has quite a large balcony. What I don't know is how much he's asking. Do you think it might interest you?

TERESA Yes, definitely! If the price is reasonable. How can we get in touch with him?

PEDRO His name is Alberto Solís, and these are his phone and contact details.

TERESA Well, thanks so much, Pedro. Let's see if we're lucky!

PEDRO I hope so. See you soon.

TERESA Yes. We'll call you. Bye.

8

Week 9

- *the preterit tense (e.g., "I spoke," "I ate"), regular and irregular verbs*
- *talking about the past: when to use the preterit and when to use the imperfect*
- *the difference between **saber** (to know how, to know a fact) and **conocer** (to know of)*
- *the superlative of adjectives and adverbs (e.g., "poorest," "biggest")*
- *uses of the neuter article **lo***
- *other uses of the definite and indefinite articles*

9.1 THE PRETERITE (E.G., "I SPOKE," "I ATE")

The preterite (sometimes called the past definite) equates to the simple past, indicating a completed action that took place at a specific time.

Here are the regular conjugations of this past tense:

hablar	comer	vivir
hablé	comí	viví
hablaste	comiste	viviste
habló	comió	vivió
hablamos	comimos	vivimos
hablasteis	comisteis	vivisteis
hablaron	comieron	vivieron

Ayer hablé con Carmen.
Yesterday I spoke to Carmen.
Comieron sopa y pescado.
They ate soup and fish.
Vivió en Madrid diez años.
He lived in Madrid ten years.

9.2 IRREGULAR VERBS IN THE PRETERITE

There is an important group of verbs that are irregular in the preterite. The endings are the same for all of them, but the stem changes. Here are three examples:

andar to walk	**hacer** to do/make	**venir** to come
and*u*ve	h*i*ce	v*i*ne
and*u*viste	h*i*ciste	v*i*niste
and*u*vo	h*i*zo	v*i*no
and*u*vimos	h*i*cimos	v*i*nimos
and*u*visteis	h*i*cisteis	v*i*nisteis
and*u*vieron	h*i*cieron	v*i*nieron

Other verbs belonging to this group are listed below, with their first-person singular preterite form:

estar (to be)	est*u*ve (I was)
decir (to say)	di*j*e (I said)
saber (to know)	s*u*pe (I knew)
poner (to put)	p*u*se (I put)
poder (to be able)	p*u*de (I was able)
conducir (to drive)	condu*j*e (I drove)
querer (to want)	qu*i*se (I wanted)
haber (to have)	h*u*be (I had [aux.])
tener (to have)	t*u*ve (I had)
traer (to bring)	tra*j*e (I brought)

No quiso abrir la puerta.
He didn't want to open the door.
Estuve enfermo dos meses.
I was ill for two months.
No pudieron venir juntos.
They weren't able to come together.

Note that the third-person plural of **decir, conducir, traer** is **dijeron, condujeron, trajeron** (the **i** of the ending is omitted after the **j**).

9

9.3 PRETERITE OF **SER** AND **IR**

In the preterite, the verbs **ser** and **ir** both have the same irregular form:

fui	**fuimos**
fuiste	**fuisteis**
fue	**fueron**

El verano pasado fui a Mallorca.
Last summer I went to Mallorca.
Fue un hombre muy famoso.
He was a very famous man.

9.4 PRETERITE OF **DAR** (TO GIVE)

di	**dimos**
diste	**disteis**
dio	**dieron**

Me dio un recado para Vd.
He gave me a message for you.
Les di veinte euros.
I gave them twenty euros.

9.5 STEM-CHANGING VERBS: PRETERITE

There is a small group of verbs ending in **-ir** that are irregular in the third-person singular and plural of the preterite. The **e** in the stem becomes **i** or the **o** becomes **u**. The rest of the tense is regular:

	3rd-pers. sing.	3rd-pers. pl.
seguir (to follow)	**siguió**	**siguieron**
pedir (to ask for)	**pidió**	**pidieron**
sentir (to feel)	**sintió**	**sintieron**
dormir (to sleep)	**durmió**	**durmieron**
morir (to die)	**murió**	**murieron**

Durmió solamente cuatro horas.
He slept only four hours.
Pidieron dos botellas de vino.
They asked for two bottles of wine.

VOCABULARY 1

dar un paseo	to go for a walk
por	along
el río	river
el sobre	envelope
pagar	to pay
la comida	meal
la tarjeta de crédito	credit card
el/la camarero/a	waiter/waitress
el kilómetro	kilometer
la hora de comer	lunchtime

Exercise 1

Translate:

1 We went for a walk along the river.
2 They didn't want to see me.
3 I put the letter in the envelope.
4 He died two years later.
5 He paid for the meal with a credit card.
6 The waiter brought us the drinks and went away.
7 They walked five kilometers looking for a garage.
8 I went out at ten o'clock and returned at lunchtime.
9 We told him that his father had arrived.
10 He didn't do anything all morning.

It's sometimes difficult for learners to decide whether to use the imperfect or the preterite because, at times, they can both translate to the English "did." Remember that the imperfect conveys what was going on—what someone was doing or used to do—over an indefinite period of time, whereas the preterite expresses what happened or what someone did at a particular point in time. The following examples show the different uses:

Nadábamos en el río todos los días.
We swam (used to swim) in the river every day.
Ayer nadamos en el río.
Yesterday we swam in the river.
Siempre fumaba un puro después de cenar.
He always smoked (used to smoke) a cigar after dinner.
Anoche fumó un puro después de cenar.
Last night he smoked a cigar after dinner.
Llovía cuando salimos del hotel.
It was raining when we left the hotel.
Llovió toda la tarde.
It rained all afternoon.

VOCABULARY 2

la ducha	shower
sonar (ue)	to sound, to ring
jugar (ue)	to play (e.g., a game)
mientras	while
bajar	to go down
la cuenta	bill
hacer la maleta	to pack
cansado	tired
la (tarjeta) postal	postcard
el/la policía	police officer
preguntar	to ask

Exercise 2

Change the infinitives in parentheses into the correct form of the imperfect or preterit as appropriate.

1 Aquella mañana Ramón (salir) de su casa a las nueve.

2 Yo (estar) en la ducha cuando (sonar) el teléfono.

3 Cuando Carmen y María (viajar) a Valencia (tener) un accidente.

4 Los niños (jugar) en el jardín cuando (empezar) a llover.

5 Juan (bajar) a pagar la cuenta, mientras yo (hacer) la maleta.

6 Mi padre siempre (sentarse) en el mismo sillón.

7 Yo (volver) a casa muy cansada.

8 (Hacer) frío cuando nosotros (llegar) a Bilbao.

9 Luis (recibir) una postal de un amigo que (vivir) en Londres.

10 El policía me (preguntar) mi nombre y dirección.

9.7 THE TWO VERBS "TO KNOW"

It is important to differentiate between the verbs **saber** and **conocer**, both meaning "to know": **saber** (to know a fact), **conocer** (to be acquainted with). For example:

No sabemos cuando llegará.
We don't know when he will arrive.
Sé que está enfermo.
I know that he is ill.
Conocemos a tu hermana muy bien.
We know your sister very well.
No conozco* esa ciudad.
I don't know that town.

*The verb **conocer** and a few others ending in **-cer** and **-cir** preceded by a vowel take a **z** before the **c** in the first-person singular of the present tense. The rest of the tense is regular.

9

conocer (to know)→ **conozco** (I know)
obedecer (to obey)→ **obedezco** (I obey)
pertenecer (to belong)→ **pertenezco** (I belong)
conducir (to drive)→ **conduzco** (I drive)
traducir (to translate)→ **traduzco** (I translate)

9.8 SUPERLATIVE OF ADJECTIVES (E.G., BIGGEST)

The superlative is formed by putting **el más, la más, los más, las más** in front of the adjective.

For example:
Este hombre es el más viejo del pueblo.
This man is the oldest in the village.
Nuestra casa es la más grande de la calle.
Our house is the biggest in the street.

When the superlative immediately follows the noun, the article is omitted:

Es el edificio más alto de Madrid.
It is the highest building in Madrid.
Es la novela más interesante que he leído.
It is the most interesting novel I have read.

9.9 SUPERLATIVE OF ADVERBS

The superlative is formed by putting **lo más** in front of the adverb. (For more about **lo**, see section 9.11.)

Hágalo (Vd.) lo más pronto posible.
Do it as soon as possible.
Les escribiré el martes lo más tarde.
I'll write to them on Tuesday at the latest.

9.10 THE ABSOLUTE SUPERLATIVE

The ending **-ísimo** added to adjectives or adverbs conveys the English "most," "extremely":

Es una mujer inteligentísima.
She is a most intelligent woman.
Es un libro aburridísimo.
It is an extremely boring book.
Llegaron al aeropuerto tardísimo.
They arrived at the airport extremely late.
Hoy me he levantado tempranísimo.
Today I got up extremely early.

VOCABULARY 3

el (teléfono) móvil	cell phone
el ordenador	computer
el (ordenador) portátil	laptop
el programa de televisión	television program
divertido	amusing
la talla	size
amable	kind
interesante	interesting
la conversación	conversation
viejo	old
la farmacia	pharmacy, drugstore
la parada de autobús	bus stop

9

Exercise 3

Translate:

1 They don't know that film.
2 He knows that I want a laptop.
3 That television program is most amusing.
4 This size is the smallest we have.
5 These shoes are the prettiest, those are the cheapest.
6 He is the kindest man I know.
7 They don't know that I want to see them.
8 It was a most interesting conversation.
9 It is the oldest church in this town.
10 The pharmacy was far from the bus stop.

9.11 USE OF THE NEUTER ARTICLE LO

We have already seen examples of **lo** preceding:

1 an adverb

Contestó lo mejor que pudo.
He answered as best he could.

2 the relative **que**

Lo que quiero decir.
What I want to say.

But **lo** may also precede an adjective, thus turning it into an abstract noun:

Lo difícil es conseguir el dinero.
The difficult thing is to obtain the money.
Lo importante es llegar a tiempo.
The important thing is to arrive on time.

USES OF THE DEFINITE AND INDEFINITE
ARTICLES

The definite article is used in Spanish in the following
cases:

1 before nouns used in a general sense

El vino es barato en España.
Wine is cheap in Spain.

2 before abstract nouns

El amor es ciego.
Love is blind.

3 before titles

La reina Isabel de Inglaterra
Queen Elizabeth of England
El señor y la señora Ruiz/Los señores Ruiz
Mr. and Mrs. Ruiz

4 before names of institutions, public places, etc.

el hospital (hospital), **la iglesia** (church),
la universidad (university)

5 before proper nouns qualified by an adjective

el pobre Carlos poor Carlos
el viejo Madrid old Madrid

6 before parts of the body and articles of clothing, when
in English the possessive "my," "his," etc., would be used

Se ha roto la pierna.
He has broken his leg.
Me pondré el abrigo azul.
I will put on my blue coat.

9

7 before days of the week, seasons, and certain expressions of time

Volveremos el martes. We will return on Tuesday.
El invierno se acerca. Winter is approaching.
Lo vi la semana pasada. I saw him last week.

8 in certain set expressions

el diez por ciento de rebaja ten percent reduction
seis euros el kilo six euros per kilo

The indefinite article is used before an abstract noun qualified by an adjective. For example:

Condujo a una velocidad increíble.
He drove at an incredible speed.

But it is not used:

1 before a noun indicating occupation, nationality, religion, or politics:

Es contable. He is an accountant.
Es española. She is Spanish.
Soy protestante. I am a Protestant.
¿Es Vd. conservador? Are you a conservative?

However, if the noun is qualified by an adjective, the article is used:

Es un buen contable. He is a good accountant.

2 before certain words:

otro (another), **cierto** (certain), **medio** (half a), **cien** (a hundred), **mil** (a thousand), **tal** (such a), **¡qué!** (what a!)

Voy a comprar otro móvil.
I am going to buy another cell phone.

cierta mujer que conozco a certain woman I know
medio litro de leche half a liter of milk
¡Qué desastre! What a disaster!

VOCABULARY 4

ponerse	to put on
el guante	glove
el/la dependiente/a	shop assistant
principal	main
preocuparse	to worry
romper(se)	to break
derecho	right
el brazo	arm
hoy día	nowadays
la dificultad	difficulty
la botella	bottle
el zumo	juice

Exercise 4

Translate:

1 Tea is a very pleasant drink.
2 Mrs. Collado will arrive on Sunday.
3 She put on her gloves because it was cold.
4 He is a waiter, and she is a shop assistant.
5 I spent two weeks in hospital.
6 The main thing is not to worry.
7 Poor Mary has broken her right arm.
8 Books are very expensive nowadays.
9 He used to walk with great difficulty.
10 He is going to bring another cup.
11 We drank half a bottle of juice.
12 The best thing is to sell the house.

9

Drill 1

Example:
Yo no quería invitar a Carmen . . . pero tuve que invitarla.
I didn't want to invite Carmen . . . but I had to invite her.

Nosotros no queríamos ir a la playa . . . pero tuvimos
   que ir.
We didn't want to go to the beach . . . but we had to go.

  1 Pedro no quería escribir la carta . . .
  2 Ellos no querían pagar la cuenta . . .
  3 Yo no quería ver a Juan . . .
  4 Nosotros no queríamos ir a la fiesta . . .
  5 (Vd.) no quería salir del hotel . . .
  6 Carmen no quería hacer la comida . . .
  7 El niño no quería comer el pescado . . .
  8 María no quería ponerse el vestido . . .
  9 Yo no quería darle mi nombre . . .
 10 Nosotras no queríamos beber el zumo . . .

9

Drill 2

Example:
¿Has hablado con Pedro hoy? Have you spoken with
   Pedro today?
No, hablé con él ayer. No, I spoke with him yesterday.

¿Han visto (Vds.) a Conchita hoy? Have you seen
   Conchita today?
No, la vimos ayer. No, we saw her yesterday.

  1 ¿Habéis estado en la playa hoy?
  2 ¿Han venido tus padres hoy?
  3 ¿Ha comprado (Vd.) este libro hoy?

4 ¿Han pagado la cuenta hoy?

5 ¿Ha recibido Juan la postal hoy?

6 ¿Habéis hecho las maletas hoy?

7 ¿Ha llovido hoy?

8 ¿Han traído las flores hoy?

9 ¿Han ido (Vds.) al museo hoy?

10 ¿Has visitado a tus amigos hoy?

Drill 3

Example:
Es una catedral muy grande. It's a very large cathedral.
Sí, es la más grande que he visto. Yes, it's the largest
  I've seen.

1 Es un vestido muy bonito.

2 Son unos libros muy caros.

3 Es una playa muy grande.

4 Es un hotel muy elegante.

5 Son unos programas muy divertidos.

6 Son unas ventanas muy pequeñas.

9

Juan y Paloma hablan de lo que han hecho durante el fin de semana.

JUAN El sábado me levanté muy tarde porque estaba cansadísimo de trabajar tanto durante la semana.

PALOMA ¿A qué le llamas tú tarde?

JUAN A las doce y media o la una. Era casi la hora de comer. Mi mujer no estaba muy contenta porque quería ir de compras conmigo por la mañana.

PALOMA Así que, tuviste que ir por la tarde.

JUAN Claro. Y fue larguísimo porque las tiendas estaban llenas de gente. Así que cuando volvimos, mi mujer preparó una cena rápida y nos sentamos a ver la televisión hasta las once y media.

PALOMA Yo fui a una boda el sábado. Se casaba un primo mío.

JUAN ¿Te divertiste?

PALOMA Sí, estuvo muy bien. La comida fue buenísima, y la bebida también, claro. Hubo música y baile hasta las tres de la mañana.

JUAN Y el domingo, ¿qué hiciste?

PALOMA Nada importante. Dormir, leer el periódico y ver la televisión ¿Y tú?

JUAN Poco más o menos, lo mismo que tú.

9

Juan and Paloma talk about what they did over the weekend.

JUAN   On Saturday I got up very late because I was exhausted after working so hard during the week.

PALOMA   What do you call late?

JUAN   Half past twelve or one o'clock. It was almost lunchtime. My wife wasn't very pleased because she wanted to go shopping with me in the morning.

PALOMA   So you had to go in the afternoon.

JUAN   That's right. And it was endless, because the shops were crowded. So when we got back, my wife prepared a quick dinner and we sat down to watch television until half past eleven.

PALOMA   I went to a wedding on Saturday. A cousin of mine was getting married.

JUAN   Did you have a good time?

PALOMA   Yes, it was great. The food was very good and the drink too, of course. There was music and dancing till three in the morning.

JUAN   And Sunday, what did you do?

PALOMA   Nothing much. Sleep, read the paper, and watch television. And you?

JUAN   More or less the same as you.

Week 10

- *the different uses of* **por** *and* **para**, *both meaning "for"*
- *the passive voice—how to form it and its avoidance in Spanish*
- *more verbs with spelling changes to preserve the original pronunciation*
- *verbs followed directly by an infinitive and verbs that take a preposition before the infinitive*

10.1 DIFFERENT USES OF **POR** AND **PARA**

It is important to learn the uses of **por** and **para**, especially as either may translate as the English "for."

The preposition **por** is used to indicate means, motive, or exchange. It translates such English prepositions as: by, through, because of, out of, for the sake of, for.

Le di las gracias por las flores.
I thanked him ("gave him thanks") for the flowers.
El ladrón entró por la ventana.
The thief came in through the window.
Lo hizo por nosotros.
She did it for us.
Envié el equipaje por tren.
I sent the luggage by train.

The preposition **para** is used to indicate purpose, suitability, or destination. It translates such English terms as: for, to, in order to, so as to.

Necesito dinero para comprar los billetes.
I need money to buy the tickets.
Este abrigo es demasiado grande para mí.
This coat is too big for me.
El tren sale para Málaga dentro de cinco minutos.
The train leaves for Malaga within five minutes.
Es un regalo para Vd.
It is a present for you.

10

There are also many idiomatic uses of **por** and **para** that you'll gradually pick up through practice. Here are some common examples:

Estamos para salir.
We are about to go out.
Estoy por no hacerlo.
I am inclined not to do it.
Lo dejaremos para mañana.
We will leave it for tomorrow.
una vez por semana once a week
por la tarde in the afternoon (evening)
por ejemplo for example
por último finally
por consiguiente therefore, consequently
por lo visto evidently

VOCABULARY 1

joven	young
el sacrificio	sacrifice
pasar	to pass
la Aduana	Customs
cobrar	to charge
el cine	cinema
las compras	purchases, shopping
la llave	key
el armario	cupboard, wardrobe
difícil	difficult
el avión	airplane
cualquier cosa	anything
la curiosidad	curiosity
el melocotón	peach

10

Exercise 1

Fill in the gaps with "por" or "para" as appropriate:

1 Pagó seiscientos euros ... el coche.
2 No podemos salir ... esa puerta.
3 Voy de vacaciones ... descansar.
4 Lo llamaré ... teléfono mañana.
5 Estas cartas no son ... mí.
6 Es demasiado joven ... comprenderlo.
7 Hizo ese sacrificio ... su padre.
8 Hay que tener mucho dinero ... viajar.
9 Saldremos ... Valencia el martes.
10 No pudo venir a la fiesta ... estar enfermo.

Exercise 2

Translate:

1 We have to pass through Customs.
2 They charged us twenty euros for the meal.
3 It's too late to go to the movies.
4 I need a bag for all my shopping.
5 Do you (pol.) have a key to open this cupboard?
6 This book is too difficult for him.
7 The plane leaves for Madrid at a quarter past seven.
8 I would do anything for him.
9 We read the letter out of curiosity.
10 She wants to buy some peaches for her mother.

10

10.2 FORMING THE PASSIVE

The passive is formed with the verb **ser** followed by the past participle. The agent is usually introduced by **por**, although **de** is sometimes used after verbs of feeling and in some set expressions, such as **cubierto de** (covered by) and **acompañado de** (accompanied by). In the passive, the past participle has to agree in gender and number with the subject.

La carta fue firmada por el presidente.
The letter was signed by the president.
El soldado fue herido por una bala.
The soldier was wounded by a bullet.

Note that the past participle is also used with **estar** to indicate state, whereas with **ser,** it indicates action. Compare the following examples:

El libro está publicado en cinco idiomas.
The book is published in five languages.
El libro será publicado en cinco idiomas.
The book will be published in five languages.

10.3 AVOIDANCE OF THE PASSIVE

The passive is less frequently used in Spanish than in English and is often avoided in the following ways:

1 By using the reflexive pronoun **se**:

Se prohíbe fumar.
Smoking is forbidden.
El museo se cierra a las seis.
The museum closes (it is closed) at six.

se also translates the English "one":

No se puede decir. One cannot say.

10

2 By using the third-person plural of the verb as an impersonal form:

Nos vieron salir de la casa.
They saw us (we were seen) leaving the house.
Dicen que no va a volver.
They say (it is said) that he is not coming back.

3 By changing the roles of subject and agent using the active voice, so that "she was shot by someone," for example, becomes "someone shot her." Thus:

Lo paró la policía.
He was stopped by the police.

VOCABULARY 2

construir	to build
el/la abuelo/a	grandfather/grandmother
acusar	to accuse
el robo	theft
el barco	boat
ahora	now
creer	to believe
muerto	dead
la montaña	mountain
cubierto	covered
la nieve	snow
la cena	dinner
servir (i)	to serve
pintar	to paint
recibir	to receive
el director/ la directora	director
presentar	to introduce
famoso	famous
el actor/ la actriz	actor/actress

10

Exercise 3

Translate:

1 The house was built by his grandfather.
2 I was accused of the theft.
3 The boat was sold for five hundred euros.
4 The work is now finished.
5 It is believed that he is dead.
6 The mountains were covered in snow.
7 Dinner is not served until nine.
8 The windows were painted three weeks ago.
9 They were received by one of the directors.
10 The program was introduced by a famous actor.

10.4 SPELLING CHANGES IN VERBS

Certain verbs have a spelling change in the stem in certain conjugations in order to preserve the original pronunciation. For example, verbs ending in:

-car change the **c** into **qu** before **e**:
buscar (to look for)→ **busqué** (I looked for)

-zar change the **z** into **c** before **e**:
empezar (to begin)→ **empecé** (I began)

-gar change the **g** into **gu** before **e**:
pagar (to pay)→ **pagué** (I paid)

-**ger** or -**gir** change the **g** into **j** before **a** or **o**:
coger (to pick up)→ **cojo** (I pick up)
dirigir (to direct)→ **dirija Vd.** (Direct! [imperative])

Note that an unaccented **i** between two vowels is always changed to **y**:

leer (to read)→ **leyó, leyeron** (he/she, they read)
creer (to think)→ **creyó, creyeron** (he/she, they thought)

10

huir (to flee)→ **huyó, huyeron** (he/she, they fled)
construir (to build)→ **construyó, construyeron**
 (he/she, they built)
oír (to hear)→ **oyó, oyeron** (he/she, they heard)
caer (to fall)→ **cayó, cayeron** (he/she, they fell)

These changes also occur in the present participle:

leyendo (reading)
creyendo (thinking)
huyendo (fleeing)
construyendo (building)
oyendo (hearing)
cayendo (falling)

VOCABULARY 3

el aparcamiento	parking lot
el ruido	noise
arriba	upstairs
secar(se)	to dry (oneself)
el pie	foot
al fuego	by the fire
el suelo	ground, floor
las instrucciones	instructions
el principio	beginning
la guerra	war
el cuadro	picture, painting
el equipaje	luggage

10

Exercise 4

Translate:

1 I played with the children all afternoon.
2 They are building a new parking lot.
3 He heard a noise upstairs.
4 I dried my feet by the fire.
5 They fell to the ground.
6 He is reading the instructions.
7 They fled from Spain at the beginning of the war.
8 I paid a lot of money for that painting.
9 Pick up the luggage, please (pol.).
10 He thought that the shop was closed.

10.5 VERBS FOLLOWED BY AN INFINITIVE

Some Spanish verbs are directly followed by an infinitive, while others take a preposition before the infinitive. The following lists include some of the most common verbs in each of these cases.

VERBS DIRECTLY FOLLOWED BY INFINITIVE

aconsejar (to advise)
Me aconsejó esperar. He advised me to wait.

conseguir (to manage to)
Conseguimos abrirlo. We managed to open it.

deber (must)
Debo visitarla más a menudo. I must visit her more often.

decidir (to decide)
Decidió venir conmigo. She decided to come with me.

esperar (to hope to)
Esperamos verlo en España.
We hope to see him in Spain.

10

intentar (to try to)
Intenté encontrar un empleo. I tried to find a job.

parecer (to appear to, to seem)
Pareció ser una falsa alarma.
It appeared to be a false alarm.

pedir (to ask to)
Ha pedido hablar con el gerente.
He has asked to speak to the manager.

pensar (to intend)
Pienso salir muy temprano.
I intend to leave very early.

poder (to be able to, can)
No podíamos ver nada.
We could not see anything.

VERBS FOLLOWED BY **A** + INFINITIVE

entrar (to come in)
Entró a preguntar el precio.
She came in to ask the price.

empezar (to begin)
Empezó a comer. He began to eat.

enseñar (to teach)
Me enseñó a conducir. She taught me to drive.

aprender (to learn)
Aprendieron a nadar enseguida.
They quickly learned to swim.

decidirse (to decide)
Me decidí a decírselo. I decided to tell him.

volver (to return)
Volvió a recoger su maleta.
He came back to collect his suitcase.

10

Note that **volver a** can be used idiomatically with the meaning of "to do something again":

Volví a verlo al día siguiente.
I saw him again the following day.

VERBS FOLLOWED BY **DE** + INFINITIVE

acabar (to finish)
Acabó de leer la carta.
She finished reading the letter.

Note that **acabar de** used in the present or imperfect indicative has the meaning of "to have just":

Acabo de ver a Juan. I have just seen John.
Acababan de salir. They had just gone out.

acordarse (to remember)
No se acordó de llevar su pasaporte.
He didn't remember to take his passport.

cansarse (to get tired)
Me cansé de andar. I got tired of walking.

dejar (to stop)
El niño dejó de llorar. The child stopped crying.

olvidarse (to forget)
Se olvidaron de comprar gasolina.
They forgot to buy gas.

tratar (to try)
Traté de verlo. I tried to see him.

VERBS FOLLOWED BY **EN** + INFINITIVE

consentir (to consent, to agree)
Ha consentido en hablar con ella.
He has agreed to speak to her.

10

insistir (to insist)
Insistió en acompañarme. He insisted on going with me.

pensar (to think)
Pensaba en escribir a su amigo.
She was thinking of writing to her friend.

vacilar (to hesitate)
Vacilé en darle la noticia.
I hesitated to tell him the news.

tardar (to take time)
Tardó mucho en llegar. He took a long time to arrive.

VERBS FOLLOWED BY **POR** + INFINITIVE

acabar (to finish, end up)
Acabé por darle el dinero.
I ended up giving him the money.

empezar (to begin)
Empezaremos por aprender el alfabeto.
We shall begin by learning the alphabet.

esforzarse (to make an effort)
Se esforzó por ser amable.
He made an effort to be kind.

VERBS FOLLOWED BY **CON** + INFINITIVE

amenazar (to threaten)
El hombre amenazó con disparar.
The man threatened to shoot.

soñar (to dream)
Sueña con ganar mucho dinero.
He dreams of making a lot of money.

contentarse (to content oneself, to be satisfied)
Me contento con descansar unos minutos.
I am content with resting for a few minutes.

VOCABULARY 4

alquilar	to hire, to rent
quejarse de	to complain
el servicio	service
jugar a	to play (a game)
el tenis	tennis
telefonear	to phone
subir	to climb
el paquete	parcel, package
la discusión	argument
sonreír (i)	to smile
ganar	to earn

Exercise 5

Translate:

1 I managed to speak with them.
2 He advised us to rent a car.
3 They tried to come into the room.
4 I intend to complain about the service.
5 We are learning to play tennis.
6 I called him up again.
7 Mr. Solís has just arrived.
8 He got tired of climbing and sat down.
9 It stopped raining, and the sun came out.
10 I forgot to give him the message.
11 They insisted on paying for their tickets.
12 The parcel took two weeks to arrive.
13 They finished by having an argument.
14 The woman made an effort to smile.
15 The man threatened to call the police.
16 He is content with earning very little.

10

Drills 1–3

Fill in the blanks with either "por" or "para" as appropriate:

1 ¿Necesitas dinero? Sí, ... comprar los sellos.

2 ¿Ha comprado el vestido? Sí, ... treinta euros.

3 ¿Llevas un libro? Sí, ... leer en la playa.

4 ¿Has comprado un regalo? Sí, ... mi madre.

5 ¿Ha enviado (Vd.) el paquete? Sí, ... avión.

6 ¿Salen (Vds.) mañana? Sí, ... Inglaterra.

7 ¿Necesitas gafas? Sí, ... leer solamente.

8 ¿Habéis dado un paseo? Sí, ... el borde del río.

Avoid the passive voice by using the reflexive pronoun "se":

El piso fue vendido. The apartment was sold.
El piso se vendió. The apartment was sold.

1 El libro fue publicado.

2 Los coches fueron alquilados.

3 La puerta fue abierta.

4 Los ruidos fueron oídos.

5 El trabajo fue terminado.

6 La casa fue construida.

7 Los barcos fueron vendidos.

8 La carta fue leída.

Example:
¿Has visto a mi hermano? Have you seen my brother?
Sí, acabo de verlo. Yes, I have just seen him.

1 ¿Has comprado los zapatos?

2 ¿Han llegado los invitados?

3 ¿Ha recibido (Vd.) las cartas?

4 ¿Habéis hecho las compras?

5 ¿Se han acostado los niños?

6 ¿Ha encontrado (Vd.) la llave?

10

Marisa y Manolo se encuentran en una cafetería.

MANOLO ¡Por fin! Creí que no venías. Llevo aquí más de media hora.

MARISA Lo siento, Manolo. Mi padre necesitaba el coche para ir a ver a unos clientes y he tenido que venir en autobús.

MANOLO Pero el autobús suele ser rápido.

MARISA Generalmente, sí. Pero hoy hemos encontrado una manifestación en la plaza de San Pedro y el autobús no podía pasar.

MANOLO Y ¿para qué era la manifestación?

MARISA No sé. No he conseguido enterarme. Pero había muchos jóvenes que no dejaban de gritar y que insistían en ponerse delante del autobús.

MANOLO ¡Siempre hay algún jaleo! Bueno, ¿qué vas a tomar?

MARISA Tengo sed. Creo que empezaré por tomar una cerveza y después, quizás, algo de comer.

MANOLO Yo acababa de tomar una ginebra con tónica cuando has llegado. Pero voy a tomar otra y un bocadillo de jamón porque tengo hambre.

MARISA ¿Qué vamos a hacer después?

MANOLO Pues había pensado ir al cine; ¿qué te parece?

MARISA Sí, buena idea. Hay varias películas que me gustaría ver.

MANOLO Ahora decidiremos. Primero voy a llamar al camarero.

10

Marisa and Manolo meet in a Spanish cafeteria.

MANOLO At last! I thought you weren't coming. I've been here more than half an hour.

MARISA I'm sorry, Manolo. My father needed the car to go and see some clients, and I had to come by bus.

MANOLO But the bus is usually quick.

MARISA Usually it is. But today we ran into a demonstration in St. Peter's Square, and the bus couldn't get through.

MANOLO And what was the demonstration for?

MARISA I don't know. I didn't manage to find out. But there were lots of young people who wouldn't stop shouting and insisted on standing in front of the bus.

MANOLO There's always some trouble! Well, what are you going to have?

MARISA I'm thirsty. I think I'll start by having a beer and then, maybe, something to eat.

MANOLO I had just had a gin and tonic when you arrived. But I'm going to have another one and a ham sandwich, because I'm hungry.

MARISA What are we going to do later?

MANOLO Well, I thought we could go to the movies. What do you think?

MARISA Yes, good idea. There are several films that I'd like to see.

MANOLO We'll decide in a minute ("presently"). First I'm going to call the waiter.

Review exercises

Exercise 1

Put the verbs in italics in the following sentences into the future tense:

1 *Vamos* de paseo después de comer.
2 Pablo *cuida* a los niños.
3 *Trabajo* dos días por semana.
4 *Se levanta* a las ocho.
5 *Salimos* a cenar con unos amigos.
6 *Viene* a vernos el domingo.
7 *Hace* buen tiempo todo el verano.
8 Se lo *dio* al camarero.
9 Este año no *pueden* ir de vacaciones.
10 Ahora *tienes* que hablar español.

Exercise 2

This deals with reported speech. Study the examples to see what you have to do and then complete the exercise:

Hablaré con el gerente. I'll speak to the manager.
Dijo que hablaría con el gerente. He said he would speak to the manager.

Hablaremos con el gerente. We'll speak to the manager.
Dijeron que hablarían con el gerente. They said they would speak to the manager.

1 Traeré las maletas. Dijo que ....
2 Volveremos a las cinco. Dijeron que ....
3 Viajaré en avión. Dijo que ....
4 Pagaremos por cheque. Dijeron que ....
5 Enviaré una postal. Dijo que ....
6 Tendrán que saberlo pronto. Dijeron que ....

10

Exercise 3

Translate:

1 Last night I saw Antonio with his wife.
2 The train arrived two hours late.
3 He offered to help me with the bags.
4 We didn't need any winter clothes.
5 They sold the house to a friend of theirs.
6 I drove 100 kilometers without stopping.
7 He went to look for a pharmacy.
8 She didn't like the book I gave her.

Exercise 4

Back home after a short holiday in Spain with your wife, you meet a Spanish friend, Alberto, who asks you what you did. Figure out what he says and then answer by translating the lines in English.

ALBERTO ¿Qué tal lo pasasteis en España?
USTED Very well. It was a very interesting journey.
ALBERTO ¿Adónde fuisteis?
USTED We went to Córdoba, Granada, and Sevilla.
ALBERTO ¡Qué bien! ¿Habíais estado antes en esas ciudades?
USTED My wife had been to Sevilla, but I didn't know any of them.
ALBERTO ¿Cuál de ellas te gustó más?
USTED I don't know. It's difficult to choose one. Each has a different beauty. Possibly Granada. The Alhambra is wonderful.
ALBERTO Sí, a mí también me gusta mucho Granada, pero de las tres prefiero Sevilla. Sevilla tiene un encanto especial para mí.
USTED Alberto, I would like to go on talking, but I have to go shopping with my wife. She'll be waiting for me. I'll call you on Friday.
ALBERTO Sí, a ver si tomamos una copa juntos. Adiós.

10

Exercise 5

Translate:

1 Why do you (fam. sing.) need the money?
2 I need it to buy a new car.
3 They left yesterday for Argentina.
4 I am doing this for you (for your sake) (fam.).
5 We are too tired to walk to the station.
6 The hotel costs fifty euros per person.
7 He invited me to his house for a month.
8 They sent me a card to tell me they were coming.

Exercise 6

These sentences are all in the passive voice. Rewrite them using one of the means of avoiding the passive given in section 10.3:

1 Los vuelos han sido cancelados.
2 Fue acompañado por su mujer.
3 La película ha sido censurada.
4 Las elecciones fueron anunciadas en octubre.
5 El muchacho fue arrestado por la policía.
6 La exposición fue inaugurada por el Rey.
7 La explosión fue oída en todo el pueblo.
8 El cheque no ha sido aceptado por el banco.

Exercise 7

Put the correct prepositions after the verbs in the following sentences, if appropriate:

1 Se cansó ... estudiar y salió ... dar un paseo.
2 Mi padre me enseñó ... nadar.
3 Intentamos ... comprar billetes, pero estaba todo vendido.
4 Me ha prometido que va ... dejar ... fumar.
5 La carta tardó ... llegar cinco días.

10

6 Al salir del cine empezó … llover.

7 Volví … telefonear, pero no contestaron.

8 Consiguió … encontrar un empleo en una fábrica.

9 Como no venía el autobús, decidimos … tomar
un taxi.

10 Acabo … leer una novela buenísima.

11 Insistieron … devolverme el dinero.

12 Espero … recibir el paquete mañana.

13 María está aprendiendo … conducir.

14 Pensamos … viajar por toda España.

15 Se olvidaron … darnos su dirección.

16 Siempre sueña … volver a su país.

Exercise 8

Translate:

1 We are all tired today.

2 My daughter wants to be a lawyer.

3 When he was ill, I used to visit him every day.

4 Don't sit (fam. sing.) in that chair, it's broken.

5 It's very hot, although all the windows are open.

6 He is sad because his best friend has died.

7 I am always at home on Sundays.

8 She is a very intelligent woman, but not very kind.

9 Who are you (pol. sing.)? I'm (m.) a friend of hers.

10 We were about to leave when he arrived.

11 They didn't give him the job because he was
too young.

12 These are not my suitcases—mine are black.

10

Exercise 9

Put the verbs in brackets into the correct form of the imperfect or the preterite as appropriate:

1 Siempre que nosotros [ir] a Italia [quedarse] en el mismo hotel.

2 El policía me [hacer] parar el coche y me [pedir] el pasaporte.

3 Les dije que no [tener] dinero y no [poder] pagar la multa.

4 Carmen le [llamar] a la oficina, pero él no [estar].

5 Nosotros [llevar] media hora esperando cuando [llegar] el tren.

6 Ellos [ir] a ver Toledo, pero [volver] pronto porque [hacer] mucho frío.

7 Cuando yo [llegar] al restaurante, mi hermana ya [estar] allí.

8 El portero me [dejar] entrar cuando le [dar] una propina.

9 El avión [salir] con mucho retraso porque [haber] niebla.

10 Pedro [trabajar] durante diez años en una oficina que [estar] cerca de mi casa.

10

Week 11

- uses of the verb **deber** + infinitive (must, should, ought), or on its own (to owe)
- **saber** and **poder**: the difference between two words with the meaning "can"
- the present and perfect subjunctive: formation and use
- the familiar imperative
- idiomatic uses of **seguir** and **valer**

11.1 USES OF THE VERB DEBER

The verb **deber** followed by an infinitive translates as the English "must":

Debemos salir temprano.
We must leave early.
No debes fumar tanto.
You mustn't smoke so much.

Used in the conditional, **deber** expresses the meaning "should" or "ought":

(Vd.) no debería hablar así.
You should not speak like that.
Deberíamos tener más cuidado.
We ought to be more careful.

Deber de followed by an infinitive translates as "must" (expressing assumption or probability):

Deben de tener mucha hambre.
They must be very hungry.
El avión debe de haber llegado ya.
The plane must have arrived already.

Used without another verb, **deber** means "to owe":

Deben mucho dinero. They owe a lot of money.

It is important not to confuse these two verbs when translating the English "can." Compare the following examples:

¿Sabe (Vd.) conducir?
Can you drive? (= Do you know how to?)
¿Puede (Vd.) conducir?
Can you drive? (= Are you physically able to?)

VOCABULARY 1

la cosa	thing
las gafas	glasses, spectacles
allí	there
a menudo	often
la explicación	explanation
el anillo	ring
costar (ue)	to cost
montar en bicicleta	to ride a bicycle
la pastilla	pill, tablet
cocinar	to cook

11

Exercise 1

Translate:

1 How much do I owe you (pol. sing.)?
2 They ought not to say those things.
3 She must have a good job.
4 I must see a doctor.
5 Can he speak Spanish?
6 I can't read without glasses.
7 We should go there more often.
8 He owes me an explanation.
9 That ring must cost a lot of money.
10 I can't ride a bicycle.
11 He can't take a pill without water.
12 Can you (fam. sing.) cook?

11.3 THE PRESENT SUBJUNCTIVE

1 Regular verbs
Here is the conjugation of the present subjunctive:

hablar	comer	vivir
hable	coma	viva
hables	comas	vivas
hable	coma	viva
hablemos	comamos	vivamos
habléis	comáis	viváis
hablen	coman	vivan

2 Stem-changing verbs
Stem-changing **-ar** and **-er** verbs have the same stem change in the subjunctive as in the present indicative:

cerrar (ie)	volver (ue)
cierre	vuelva
cierres	vuelvas

cierre	vuelva
cerremos	volvamos
cerréis	volváis
cierren	vuelvan

In the present subjunctive, stem-changing **-ir** verbs take a stem change in every person. In the first- and second-person plural, the **e** changes to **i** or **o** changes to **u**:

pedir (i)	sentir (ie)	dormir (ue)
pida	sienta	duerma
pidas	sientas	duermas
pida	sienta	duerma
pidamos	sintamos	durmamos
pidáis	sintáis	durmáis
pidan	sientan	duerman

3 Other irregular verbs
The stem of the present subjunctive of most irregular verbs is the same as that of the first-person singular of the present indicative. For instance:

	Present	Present subjunctive
tener	**tengo**	**tenga, -as, -a,** etc.
venir	**vengo**	**venga, -as, -a,** etc.
traer	**traigo**	**traiga, -as, -a,** etc.
conocer	**conozco**	**conozca, -as, -a,** etc.

The exceptions to this rule are: **dar**, **estar**, **haber**, **ir**, **saber**, and **ser**:

dar	estar	haber
dé	esté	haya
des	estés	hayas
dé	esté	haya
demos	estemos	hayamos
deis	estéis	hayáis
den	estén	hayan

ir	saber	ser
vaya	sepa	sea
vayas	sepas	seas
vaya	sepa	sea
vayamos	sepamos	seamos
vayáis	sepáis	seáis
vayan	sepan	sean

To differentiate the first- and third-person singular of the present subjunctive, the subject pronoun is often used.

11.4 THE PRESENT PERFECT SUBJUNCTIVE

The present perfect subjunctive is formed with the present subjunctive of **haber** + a past participle:

... que hayan salido ...
... that they may have gone out ...
... que hayamos visto ...
... that we may have seen ...

11.5 USES OF THE SUBJUNCTIVE

The subjunctive is generally used in dependent clauses in which the action of the verb is presented not as a reality but as a possibility: something that is yet to happen. It is used:

1 after verbs expressing a wish, command, request, need, permission, prohibition, preference, doubt, emotion

For example:
Quieren que cantemos. They want us to sing.
Necesito que me ayudes. I need you to help me.
Prefiero que (Vd.) lo haga. I prefer you to do it.
Me prohíben que vaya. They forbid me to go.
Siento que estés enfermo. I'm sorry you are ill.

11

Note that when the subject of the dependent verb is the same as that of the main verb, the infinitive is used rather than the subjunctive:

Quieren cantar. They want to sing.
Prefiero hacerlo. I prefer to do it.

2 after impersonal expressions that indicate doubt, preference, possibility, probability, necessity

Es preferible que esperemos. It's preferable that we wait.
Es dudoso que vengan. It's doubtful that they will come.
Es posible que lo sepa. It's possible that he knows it.

3 after certain conjunctions when they introduce an uncertain or future action

Se lo daré cuando lo vea.
I'll give it to him when I see him.
Tendrán que pagarlo aunque no quieran.
They'll have to pay for it even if they don't want to.

4 after the following related phrases

antes de que	before
hasta que	until
para que	so as to
sin que	without
con tal que	provided that
a no ser que	unless
después de que	after

Lo terminaré antes de que llegue.
I'll finish it before he arrives.
Saldremos sin que nos vean.
We'll go out without their seeing us.

5 after relative pronouns with indefinite negative or interrogative antecedents

¿Hay alguien que sepa dónde está?
Is there anyone who knows where it is?
No hay un hombre que no quiera triunfar.
There is not a man who doesn't want to succeed.

6 after the following expressions when they introduce a future action

quienquiera, quienesquiera	whoever
cualquiera, cualesquiera	whatever
comoquiera	however
cuandoquiera	whenever
dondequiera	wherever

No quiero verlo, quienquiera que sea.
I don't want to see him, whoever he is.
Dondequiera que vaya, siempre llevo mi pasaporte.
Wherever I go, I always carry my passport.

"However" followed by an adjective or an adverb is always rendered in Spanish by **por** + adjective/adverb + the subjunctive:

Por mucho que lo quieras.
However much you love him.
Por caros que sean.
However expensive they may be.
Por estúpido que parezca.
However stupid it may seem.

VOCABULARY 2

alegrarse	to be glad
el/la abogado/a	lawyer
el documento	document
mandar	to order
dudar	to doubt
sorprender	to surprise
perderse	to lose one's way
la lástima	pity

dejar	to let, to allow
el precio	price
tocar	to play (an instrument)
el piano	piano
cuidar de	to look after
el problema	problem
tener éxito	to succeed
la práctica	practice

Exercise 2

Translate (in sentences with "you," use the fam. sing.):

1 I am glad they are able to come.
2 He wants the lawyer to see the documents.
3 They have ordered us to wait here.
4 I doubt that the sun will come out.
5 It surprises me that she has not written.
6 He has asked me to teach him Spanish.
7 It's possible that they have lost their way.
8 It's a pity that we haven't enough money.
9 It's probable that they will get married.
10 I won't be able to do it unless they help me.
11 We'll go to the movies, provided you let me pay.
12 He will wait until I return.
13 They will have to eat it, even if they don't like it.
14 There is no one who can pay that price.
15 Is there anyone who can play the piano?
16 I need someone to look after the children.
17 We'll find it, wherever it is.
18 He will help you whenever you have a problem.
19 However much he may try, he will never succeed.
20 However easy it may seem, one needs practice.

11

The familiar imperative is used in contexts in which you address someone with **tú** (sing.) or **vosotros** (pl.), whereas the polite imperative, which we've already seen, corresponds to **Vd.** and **Vds.**

1 Regular verbs

hablar	**habla (tú)**	**hablad (vosotros)**	speak!
comer	**come (tú)**	**comed (vosotros)**	eat!
vivir	**vive (tú)**	**vivid (vosotros)**	live!

2 Stem-changing verbs: only the singular is irregular

cerrar	**cierra (tú)**	**cerrad (vosotros)**	close!
volver	**vuelve (tú)**	**volved (vosotros)**	come back!
pedir	**pide (tú)**	**pedid (vosotros)**	ask!

3 Irregular verbs: only the singular is irregular

decir	**di (tú)**	**decid (vosotros)**	say!
hacer	**haz (tú)**	**haced (vosotros)**	do!, make!
ir	**ve (tú)**	**id (vosotros)**	go!
oír	**oye (tú)**	**oíd (vosotros)**	hear!
poner	**pon (tú)**	**poned (vosotros)**	put!
salir	**sal (tú)**	**salid (vosotros)**	go out!
ser	**sé (tú)**	**sed (vosotros)**	be!
tener	**ten (tú)**	**tened (vosotros)**	have!
venir	**ven (tú)**	**venid (vosotros)**	come!

The familiar imperative only exists in the positive. To tell someone not to do something, the second-person singular and plural of the present subjunctive are used.

No hables. (sing.)	**No habléis.** (pl.)	Don't speak.
No cierres. (sing.)	**No cerréis.** (pl.)	Don't close.
No vayas. (sing.)	**No vayáis.** (pl.)	Don't go.

Object and reflexive pronouns are attached to the end of the verb in the positive imperative, but they precede the verb in the negative imperative.

11

Míralo. (sing.)	**Miradlo.** (pl.)	Look at it.
No lo mires. (s.)	**No lo miréis.** (pl.)	Don't look at it.
Siéntate. (sing.)	**Sentaos.** (pl.)	Sit down.
No te sientes. (s.)	**No os sentéis.** (pl.)	Don't sit down.

Note that the final **-d** of the plural form is omitted when the reflexive pronoun is attached. The exception is **idos** (go away!) from the verb **ir**. Note also that in some cases, an accent is used to preserve the original stress.

Exercise 3

Put the following verbs into the familiar imperative in both positive and negative forms in the singular (for extra practice, you could do the plural forms too):

1 hacerlo

2 venir

3 acostarse

4 aprender

5 ponerlo

6 escribirla

7 gritar

8 oírlo

9 preocuparse

10 dormirse

VOCABULARY 3

enfadarse	to get angry
escuchar	to listen
vestirse (i)	to get dressed
callarse	to be quiet
despertar (ie)	to wake up
perdonar	to forgive
el error	error
mover (ue)	to move

11

Exercise 4

Translate using the familiar imperative:

1 Don't get angry. (s.)
2 Listen to me. (pl.)
3 Get dressed. (s.)
4 Don't tell me that. (pl.)
5 Be careful. (pl.)
6 Read it to us. (s.)
7 Be quiet. (pl.)
8 Don't wake me up early. (s.)
9 Forgive my error. (pl.)
10 Don't move the car. (s.)

11.7 IDIOMATIC USE OF **SEGUIR**

On its own, this verb means "to follow" or "to continue."
When it is used with the present participle of another
verb, it conveys the meaning "to keep doing something":

El perro siguió a su amo.
The dog followed his master.
Siga (Vd.) trabajando.
Keep working.

"To go on doing something" can also be rendered by the
verb **continuar** followed by the present participle:

La mujer continuó hablando.
The woman went on talking.

11.8 IDIOMATIC USE OF **VALER**

This verb can mean "to cost" or "to be worth":

¿Cuánto vale el billete?
How much does the ticket cost?

Esta pulsera no vale nada.
This bracelet is worthless.
No vale la pena.
It isn't worth it.

The verb **valer** has exactly the same irregularities in its conjugation as **salir**.

Drills 1–2

Example:
¿Tiene mucho dinero?   Does he have a lot of money?
Sí, debe de tener mucho dinero.
Yes, he must have a lot of money.

1 ¿Está enfermo?

2 ¿Son las cinco?

3 ¿Están muy tristes?

4 ¿Trabaja mucho?

5 ¿Hace muchos años?

6 ¿Están en casa?

Example:
¿Vamos a esperar?   Are we going to wait?
Sí, es preferible que esperemos.
Yes, it's better if we wait.

1 ¿Van a comer?

2 ¿Va a irse?

3 ¿Vamos a volver?

4 ¿Van a acostarse?

5 ¿Va a pagar?

6 ¿Vamos a sentarnos?

11

Drills 3–4

Example:
¿Cierro la puerta? Shall I shut the door?
Sí, ciérrala. Yes, shut it.

1 ¿Pedimos los cafés?
2 ¿Traigo el vino?
3 ¿Llamamos a Miguel?
4 ¿Compro el regalo?
5 ¿Abrimos las ventanas?
6 ¿Ayudo a Pedro?

Example:
¿Han terminado de hablar? Have they finished talking?
No, siguen hablando. No, they're still talking.

1 ¿Han terminado de comer?
2 ¿Ha terminado Juan de leer el periódico?
3 ¿Han terminado (Vds.) de trabajar?
4 ¿Ha terminado (Vd.) de pintar?
5 ¿Ha terminado Conchita de cantar?
6 ¿Han terminado de construir la casa?

11

La Sra. Ramos habla con su hijo Pablo, de
quince años.

SRA. RAMOS	Pablo, levántate, que ya son las diez y media.
PABLO	Déjame dormir un poco más. Es sábado y no tengo que ir al colegio.
SRA. RAMOS	No, pero necesito que vayas a hacerme unas compras.
PABLO	¿Por qué?
SRA. RAMOS	Porque yo no tengo tiempo de salir. Vienen unos invitados a cenar esta noche y tengo mucho que hacer en casa.
PABLO	Y ¿adónde tengo que ir?
SRA. RAMOS	Quiero que me traigas unas cosas del supermercado (ahora te haré una lista), y que recojas la carne de la carnicería.
PABLO	Espero que no me lleve mucho tiempo hacer todo eso.
SRA. RAMOS	Pues, cuanto antes te levantes, antes te pondrás en camino.
PABLO	¡Y yo que quería jugar al fútbol con mis amigos esta mañana!
SRA. RAMOS	¡Vamos! Date prisa y tendrás tiempo para todo. Ya te he puesto el desayuno en la mesa.

11

Mrs. Ramos talks with her fifteen-year-old son, Pablo.

MRS. RAMOS Pablo, get up. It's already half past ten.

PABLO Let me sleep a bit longer. It's Saturday and I don't have to go to school.

MRS. RAMOS No, but I need you to go and do some shopping for me.

PABLO Why?

MRS. RAMOS Because I don't have time to go out. Some guests are coming to dinner this evening, and I have a lot to do in the house.

PABLO And where do I have to go?

MRS. RAMOS I want you to get me a few things from the supermarket—I'll make you a list now—and to pick up the meat from the butcher's.

PABLO I hope it doesn't take me long to do all that.

MRS. RAMOS Well, the sooner you get up, the sooner you'll be on your way.

PABLO And I wanted to play soccer with my friends this morning!

MRS. RAMOS Come on! Hurry up, and you'll have time for everything. I've already put your breakfast on the table.

Week 12

- *the imperfect and past perfect subjunctive: formation and use*
- *use of the subjunctive in "if" clauses and main clauses*
- *"may" and "might"*
- *verbs followed by prepositions*
- **al** *followed by the infinitive*

12.1 THE IMPERFECT SUBJUNCTIVE

The imperfect subjunctive has two forms, with different endings. The stem is obtained by removing the ending **-ron** from the third-person plural of the preterit: **habla-, comie-, vivie-,** etc. The following endings are added to this stem: either **-ra, -ras, -ra, -ramos, -rais, -ran** or **-se, -ses, -se, semos, -seis, -sen**. Both forms are equally acceptable. It is very much a matter of choice whether one or the other is used.

1 Regular verbs

hablar	**hablara, hablaras,** etc.
	hablase, hablases, etc.
comer	**comiera, comieras,** etc.
	comiese, comieses, etc.
vivir	**viviera, vivieras,** etc.
	viviese, vivieses, etc.

2 Stem-changing verbs

cerrar	**cerrara, cerraras,** etc.
	cerrase, cerrases, etc.
volver	**volviera, volvieras,** etc.
	volviese, volvieses, etc.
pedir	**pidiera, pidieras,** etc.
	pidiese, pidieses, etc.

3 Irregular verbs

estar	**estuviera, estuvieras,** etc.
	estuviese, estuvieses, etc.

12

tener	tuviera, tuvieras, etc.
	tuviese, tuvieses, etc.
decir	dijera, dijeras, etc.
	dijese, dijeses, etc.

12.2 PAST PERFECT SUBJUNCTIVE

This tense is formed with the imperfect subjunctive of **haber** followed by the past participle of the verb:

Hubiera (hubiese) visto ...
He might have seen ...
Hubiéramos (hubiésemos) vendido ...
We might have sold ...

12.3 USES OF THE IMPERFECT AND PAST PERFECT SUBJUNCTIVE

These verb forms are used in the same contexts as the present and present perfect subjunctive (although to refer to the past), but they generally follow a different tense in the main clause. Compare the following examples:

Quiere que lo compres.
He wants you to buy it.
Quería que lo compraras.
He wanted you to buy it.
Espero que haya llegado.
I hope she has arrived.
Esperaba que hubiera llegado.
I hoped she had arrived.
Me dice que le escriba.
He tells me to write to him.
Me dijo que le escribiera.
He told me to write to him.
Es importante que lo haga.
It's important that she does it.
Era importante que lo hiciese.
It was important that she did it.

12

12.4 SEQUENCE OF TENSES

The present and present perfect subjunctive usually follow the present indicative, the future, the imperative, and the present perfect.

The imperfect and past perfect subjunctive usually follow the imperfect indicative, the preterit, the conditional, and the past perfect.

Occasionally the imperfect and past perfect subjunctive may follow a verb in the present indicative:

Siento mucho que no pudiera venir.
I'm very sorry that she couldn't come.
No es posible que lo supieran.
It's not possible that they knew.
No creo que nos hubieran invitado.
I don't think they would have invited us.

VOCABULARY 1

viajar	to travel
el accidente	accident
poner la mesa	to set the table
darse prisa	to hurry
esperar	to hope
avisar	to warn
usar	to use
la máquina	machine
reservar	to reserve, to book
la persona	person
traducir	to translate
ganar	to win
el premio	prize

12

Exercise 1

Translate:

1 They wanted me to travel with them.
2 I was afraid that he might have had an accident.
3 She told us to set the table.
4 I asked him to hurry up.
5 We hoped that it would not be too hot in Seville.
6 Wherever he went, he always found friends.
7 I warned him not to use that machine.
8 He called me so that I would book the rooms.
9 They were looking for a person who could translate the letter.
10 I am glad that they won first prize.

12.5 USE OF THE SUBJUNCTIVE IN "IF" CLAUSES

The subjunctive is used in an "if" clause when the action of the verb is uncertain or hypothetical:

Lo compraría si tuviese el dinero.
I would buy it if I had the money.
Acabaríamos antes si me ayudaras.
We would finish sooner if you helped me.

When the action of the verb can be fulfilled, the indicative is used:

Lo compraré si tengo el dinero.
I'll buy it if I have the money.
Acabaremos antes si me ayudas.
We'll finish sooner if you help me.

When the main verb is in the conditional perfect in English, in Spanish, it is often replaced by the **-ra** form of the past perfect subjunctive:

No lo hubiera insultado si no me hubiese provocado.
I would not have insulted him if he had not provoked me.

The future and conditional are not used with **si** except when it means "whether":

No sé si vendrá. I don't know whether she will come.
No me dijo si lo vendería.
He didn't tell me whether he would sell it.

VOCABULARY 2

el perro	dog	**quedarse**	to stay
morder (ue)	to bite	**más tiempo**	longer
asustar	to scare	**el paraguas**	umbrella
guardar	to keep	**mojarse**	to get
el bolsillo	pocket		wet
divertirse (ie)	to have a good time	**el concierto**	concert

Exercise 2

Translate (use the fam. sing. for "you," unless indicated otherwise):

1 I would do it if I could.
2 If the weather is good, I'll work in the garden.
3 The dog would not have bitten you if you hadn't scared it.
4 If you asked them, they wouldn't know what to say.
5 If I saw him now, I wouldn't speak to him.
6 You (pol. sing.) would not have lost the money if you had kept it in your pocket.
7 If they came to the party, they would have a good time.
8 I'll write to you if I have to stay there longer.
9 If you don't take an umbrella, you'll get wet.
10 I would go to the concert if he'd come with me.

12

USE OF THE SUBJUNCTIVE IN MAIN CLAUSES

The subjunctive is used:

1 in all imperatives, except the positive familiar imperative

Hable (Vd.). / Hablen (Vds.). (polite)
Speak.
No hable (Vd.). / No hablen (Vds.). (polite)
No hables. / No habléis. (familiar)
Don't speak.
but
Habla. / Hablad. Speak. (familiar)

2 to express a wish

¡Que tenga (Vd.) buen viaje! Have a good journey!
¡Que te mejores! Get well soon!
¡Que sean muy felices! May they be very happy!

3 after the word **ojalá** ("if only," "would that …")

¡Ojalá pudiera verlo!
If only I could see him!
¡Ojalá ganáramos la lotería!
Would that we won the lottery!

4 after **quizá(s), tal vez, acaso** ("perhaps"). Sometimes the indicative is used, depending on the degree of doubt

Quizá no venga hoy.
Perhaps he won't come today.
Acaso no lo sepan.
Perhaps they don't know it.
Tal vez no habían oído la noticia.
Perhaps they hadn't heard the news.

5 in certain set expressions

Sea como sea ... Be that as it may ...
Sea lo que sea ... Whatever it is ...
Pase lo que pase ... Whatever happens ...

12

Diga lo que diga ... Whatever he/she says ...
Hagan lo que hagan ... Whatever they do ...

6 to translate the English "let"

Que espere. Let him wait.
Que paguen. Let them pay.

12.7 "MAY" AND "MIGHT"

When they indicate possibility, "may" and "might" can be translated by any of the following expressions:

puede que, es posible que, quizá(s), tal vez: may
pudiera, era posible que, quizá(s), tal vez: might

Puede que estén trabajando. They may be working.
Es posible que llueva. It may rain.
Pensó que pudiera haber ocurrido.
He thought that it might have happened.
Dijo que era posible que volvieran.
She said that they might return.

When "may" and "might" are used to express permission, they are translated by the present or imperfect indicative:

¿Puedo entrar? May I come in?
Dijeron que podíamos jugar con ellos. They said we could play with them.

VOCABULARY 3	
perder	to miss (a train, boat, etc.)
estar en contacto con	to be in touch with
la fotografía	photograph
el día libre	day off
el aviso	warning (sign)

12

Exercise 3

Translate:

1 If only I didn't have to work.
2 Perhaps he is ill.
3 We may have missed the train.
4 Let him come if he likes.
5 If only we could have a holiday.
6 Whatever happens, I'll be in touch with you (pol.).
7 May we see the photographs?
8 He said that I could have the day off.
9 Have a good time! (fam. sing.)
10 Perhaps they didn't see the warning sign.

12.8 VERBS FOLLOWED BY PREPOSITIONS

In section 10.5, we saw some common verbs that need a preposition before an infinitive. Here are some verbs that need a preposition before the object of the verb.

acercarse a (to approach, to go near)
El hombre se acercó a la casa.
The man approached the house.

asomarse a (to lean out of)
La niña se asomó a la ventana.
The girl leaned out of the window.

casarse con (to marry)
Por fin se casó con ella.
In the end he did marry her.

contar con (to count on, to rely on)
No puedo contar con mi hermano.
I cannot rely on my brother.

dar a (to overlook)
Los balcones daban al mar.
The balconies overlooked the sea.

depender de (to depend on)
El resultado no depende de mí.
The result does not depend on me.

despedirse de (to say goodbye to)
Vinieron a despedirse de nosotros.
They came to say goodbye to us.

dudar de (to doubt)
No dude (Vd.) de su palabra.
Do not doubt his word.

enamorarse de (to fall in love with)
Se enamoró de su vecina.
He fell in love with his neighbor.

encontrarse con (to meet, to come across)
Me encontré con un viejo amigo.
I came across an old friend.

enterarse de (to find out, to hear about)
No me había enterado de su muerte.
I had not heard about his death.

fijarse en (to notice)
¿Te has fijado en el sombrero de Anita?
Have you noticed Anita's hat?

ocuparse de (to attend to)
Nos ocuparemos de los invitados.
We'll attend to the guests.

parecerse a (to resemble, to look like)
No se parece a su padre.
He doesn't look like his father.

pensar en (to think of)
Siempre está pensando en sus hijos.
He is always thinking of his children.

12

pensar de (to think of, to have an opinion on)
¿Qué piensas de esa película?
What do you think of that film?

saber a (to taste of)
Este pastel sabe a canela.
This cake tastes of cinnamon.

soñar con (to dream of)
Anoche soñé contigo.
Last night I dreamed of you.

VOCABULARY 4

el borde	edge
la ventanilla	window (of a vehicle)
concurrido	busy, crowded
el éxito	success
la obra (de teatro)	play
el/la compañero/a	colleague, companion
la buena intención	goodwill
tonto	silly
fácil	easy
el/la turista	tourist
el nombre	name
la situación	situation
el helado	ice cream
la fresa	strawberry
el lugar	place

12

Exercise 4

Translate:

1 Don't go near the edge (fam. sing.).
2 He leaned out of the car window.
3 My brother is going to marry an English woman.
4 You (fam. sing.) know that you can count on me.
5 The window overlooked a very busy street.
6 The success of the play depends on the actors.
7 I have to say goodbye to my colleagues.
8 They don't doubt his goodwill.
9 Maria has fallen in love with a very silly man.
10 It's very easy to meet American tourists in Spain.
11 We haven't been able to find out his name.
12 I didn't notice what she was wearing.
13 You (fam. sing.) have to attend to the drinks.
14 This house looks very much like ours.
15 He doesn't want to think about all the problems.
16 We don't know what he thinks of the situation.
17 This ice cream tastes of strawberry.
18 I was dreaming of all the places I had visited.

12.9 AL FOLLOWED BY THE INFINITIVE

This translates the English "on" + present participle:

Lo vi al salir del hotel.
I saw him on leaving the hotel.
Al entrar en el cuarto, todo el mundo dejó de hablar.
On entering the room, everyone stopped talking.

It can also translate sentences with "when" and "as":

Sonrió al verme.
She smiled when she saw me.
Lo saludé con la mano al entrar.
I waved at him as I came in.

12

Drills 1–2

Example:
¿Va a venir? Is he going to come?
Puede que venga. He may come.

1 ¿Va (Vd.) a venderlo?
2 ¿Van a casarse?
3 ¿Vais a salir?
4 ¿Va a volver?
5 ¿Van a invitarnos?
6 ¿Vas a nadar?

Change the verb in the future into the conditional, followed by the appropriate form of the subjunctive.

For example:
Lo compraré si tengo dinero.
I will buy it if I have the money.

Lo compraría si tuviera dinero.
I would buy it if I had the money.

1 Vendrán si pueden.
2 Lo pediremos si lo necesitamos.
3 Comeré si tengo hambre.
4 Se lo diremos si lo vemos.
5 Saldrán si no llueve.
6 Te lo daré si lo encuentro.
7 Trabajará más si le pagan bien.
8 Hablaré con ellos si vienen.

Drill 3

Example:
Se pararon cuando llegaron al puente.
They stopped when they arrived at the bridge.
Se pararon al llegar al puente.
They stopped on arriving at the bridge.

1 Se sorprendió cuando oyó la noticia.
2 Gritaron cuando vieron a los policías.
3 Lloraba cuando leía la carta.
4 Me pidió la llave cuando salía.
5 Tuve miedo cuando oí un ruido.
6 Se lavaron las manos cuando terminaron.
7 Me quité el sombrero cuando entré.
8 Empezó a llover cuando llegamos a casa.

12

Una invitación a cenar

[El teléfono suena.]

ALFONSO **¡Dígame!**

PILAR **¿Eres Alfonso?**

ALFONSO **Sí. ¿Quién es?**

PILAR **Soy Pilar.**

ALFONSO **¡Hola, Pilar! No te había conocido. ¿Cómo estás?**

PILAR **Muy bien. ¿Y tú?**

ALFONSO **Bien, gracias. ¿Querías hablar con Conchita? Ha ido a recoger a los niños al colegio.**

PILAR **¡Ah! Bueno, no importa. La razón por la que llamo es para ver si tú y Conchita queréis venir a cenar el viernes.**

ALFONSO **El viernes no podemos porque llega mi madre de Barcelona a pasar unos días con nosotros, y tenemos que ir al aeropuerto a las nueve de la noche. Lo siento mucho, Pilar.**

PILAR **No te preocupes. ¿Podéis venir el sábado?**

ALFONSO **El sábado, sí. Lo único es que no me gustaría dejar sola a mi madre.**

PILAR **Pues que venga también. Encantada de tener una invitada más.**

ALFONSO **En ese caso, estupendo. ¿A qué hora nos esperas?**

PILAR **¿Te parece bien a las ocho? Así tenemos tiempo de tomar un aperitivo antes de cenar.**

ALFONSO **Muy bien. Se lo diré a Conchita. Hasta el sábado y gracias.**

PILAR **De nada. Adiós.**

12

TRANSLATION

An invitation to dinner

[The phone rings.]

ALFONSO Hello?

PILAR Is that Alfonso?

ALFONSO Yes. Who's this?

PILAR It's Pilar.

ALFONSO Hi, Pilar! I didn't recognize your voice. How are you?

PILAR Great. And you?

ALFONSO Fine, thanks. Did you want to speak to Conchita? She's gone to pick up the children from school.

PILAR Oh! Well, it doesn't matter. The reason I'm calling is to see if you and Conchita would like to come to dinner on Friday.

ALFONSO We can't on Friday because my mother is coming from Barcelona to spend a few days with us, and we have to go to the airport at nine o'clock in the evening. I'm sorry, Pilar.

PILAR Don't worry. Can you come on Saturday?

ALFONSO On Saturday, yes. The only thing is I wouldn't want (lit. "like") to leave my mother on her own.

PILAR Well, she can come (lit. "that she come") too. Delighted to have one more guest.

ALFONSO In that case, super. What time do you expect us?

PILAR Is eight o'clock all right for you? That way we'll have time to have a drink before dinner.

ALFONSO Perfect. I'll tell Conchita. Till Saturday, and thank you.

PILAR Not at all. Bye.

12

Week 13

- how to use some important verbs in different contexts
- **más** and **menos**
- **tan** and **tal**
- **pero** and **sino**
- more prepositions
- augmentatives and diminutives
- idiomatic uses of certain verbs

13.1 SOME IMPORTANT VERBS

The following useful verbs can have different meanings in different contexts. Some of these are quite different from English usage. Here are some examples:

asistir (to assist, to attend)
Tuve que asistir al herido.
I had to assist the injured man.
Asistimos a una representación de Aída.
We attended a performance of Aida.

bastar (to be enough, to suffice)
No basta decírselo.
It's not enough to tell him.
Este pan nos basta para el desayuno.
This bread is enough for our breakfast.

caber (to fit in)
No cabemos todos en un coche.
We don't all fit into one car.
Este armario no cabe en esa habitación.
This wardrobe does not fit into that room.

devolver (to return, to give back)
Me ha devuelto mi carta. He has returned my letter.
Nos devolvieron el dinero. They refunded our money.

echar (to throw, to pour)
Eché la carta al fuego. I threw the letter on the fire.
Echó el té en la taza. She poured the tea in the cup.

faltar (to lack, to be missing)
No le falta inteligencia.
He doesn't lack intelligence.
Faltan dos páginas en este libro.
There are two pages missing in this book.

hacer falta (to need)
No hace falta ir más lejos. There's no need to go further.
Me hace falta más gasolina. I need more gas.

meter (to put in, to insert)
Metió la llave en la cerradura.
She put the key in the lock.
Me metí la mano en el bolsillo.
I put my hand in my pocket.

quedar (to remain, to have left)
Quedan cuatro lecciones. There remain four lessons.
Me quedan cuarenta dólares. I have forty dollars left.

quitar(se) (to take away, to take off)
Le quitaron el pasaporte. They took his passport.
Me quité los zapatos. I took off my shoes.

sobrar (to have more than enough, to have to spare)
Sobran candidatos para ese trabajo.
There are more than enough candidates for that job.
¿Te sobra algo de dinero?
Do you have any money to spare?

tocar (to touch, to play an instrument)
No toque (Vd.) la pintura.
Don't touch the paint.
Toca la guitarra maravillosamente.
She plays the guitar beautifully.

tomar (to take, to have food or drink)
Tomó al niño en sus brazos.
He took the child in his arms.
Vamos a tomar un café.
Let's have a coffee.

13

VOCABULARY 1

la gente	people	el/la ayudante	helper
el entierro	funeral	la silla	chair
la cantidad	amount	la chaqueta	jacket
la harina	flour	el huevo	egg
la caja	box	la tortilla	omelet
el maletero	car trunk	la seda	silk
prestar	to lend	el violín	violin
la pelota	ball	firmar	to sign
el estante	shelf		

Exercise 1

Translate:

1 Many people attended the funeral.
2 This amount of flour will be enough.
3 That box doesn't fit in the trunk of the car.
4 I want to return the magazine he lent me.
5 He threw the ball to the children.
6 I'm going to pour the wine.
7 They lack experience.
8 There are five books missing from this shelf.
9 We need more helpers.
10 They will put all the clothes in one suitcase.
11 How many days do you (fam. sing.) have left?
12 He'll take away these chairs.
13 May I take off my jacket?
14 There are more than enough eggs to make the omelet.
15 It's very pleasant to touch silk.
16 He would like to play the violin.
17 He took the pen and signed the letter.
18 They like to have wine with their meal.

13

13.2 MÁS AND MENOS

We've already seen these two words in the comparatives
más que (more than) and **menos que** (less than). But
when "more than" and "less than" are followed by a
number, they are translated by **más de** and **menos de**.

For example:
Hay más de quinientos alumnos en esa escuela.
There are more than 500 students in that school.
He pagado menos de tres euros.
I paid less than three euros.

In the negative, **que** replaces **de**, and **no ... más que** is
translated by "only":

No tengo más que un hermano.
I have only one brother.
No hay más que tres manzanas.
There are only three apples.

When **más de** and **menos de** are followed by a clause,
the forms **el que, la que, los que, las que** must be
used. If no definite noun is referred to, **lo que** is used.

For example:
Tenemos más comida de la que necesitamos.
We have more food than we need.
Es más inteligente de lo que parece.
He is more intelligent than he looks.

13.3 TAN AND TAL

Both words translate the English "such," but **tan**
precedes an adjective, whereas **tal** precedes a singular
noun (it becomes **tales** with a plural noun).

Es un libro tan interesante. It's such an interesting book.
No conozco a tal hombre. I don't know such a man.

13

Tan is also used in exclamations:

¡Qué casa tan bonita!
What a lovely house!
¡Qué día tan horrible!
What a horrible day!

The adjective **semejante** can also translate "such":

No diga (Vd.) semejante cosa.
Don't say such a thing.

13.4 PERO AND SINO

Although "but" is generally translated by **pero**, remember to use **sino** after a negative statement when "but" introduces a clause that is contrary to the first statement:

Este regalo no es para mi madre, sino para mi hermana.
This present is not for my mother, but for my sister.
No he pedido carne, sino pescado.
I haven't ordered meat, but fish.

VOCABULARY 2	
heredar	to inherit
el collar	necklace
feo	ugly
el edificio	building
aburrido	boring
listo	clever

Exercise 2

Translate:

1 He has inherited more than a million euros.
2 I can't sell it for less than a hundred euros.
3 We have lived in Madrid more than fifteen years.
4 I'll do it in less than five minutes.
5 He had never seen such a beautiful necklace.
6 What an ugly building!
7 He wouldn't do such a thing.
8 I find such books very boring.
9 That's not my brother, but my cousin.
10 They don't have a dog, but they have two cats.
11 He has more money than he says.
12 They are cleverer than you (fam. sing.) think.
13 What a good idea!
14 It's such a long journey!

13.5 PREPOSITIONS

The following are some of the most common simple and compound prepositions (**por** and **para** are not included, as they are covered in section 10.1).

a (to, at)
Used for "at" in expressions of time and a few set phrases, such as **a la mesa** (at the table) and **a la puerta** (at the door).

Van a la playa.
They're going to the beach.
Te veré a las ocho.
I'll see you at eight.
Nos sentamos a la mesa.
We sat at the table.

ante (before)
When meaning "in the presence of," "faced with."

Ante ese problema, no supo que hacer.
Faced with that problem, she didn't know what to do.
Se presentó ante el tribunal.
He appeared before the court.

antes de (before, when referring to time)
Llegaremos antes de las cuatro.
We'll arrive before four o'clock.

bajo (under)
Trabaja bajo su dirección.
He works under him.

debajo de (under, underneath)
Encontré el anillo debajo del sillón.
I found the ring under the armchair.

con (with)
Iremos con Juan. We'll go with John.
¿Quieres venir conmigo?
Do you want to come with me?

contra (against)
Ponga (Vd.) esa silla contra la pared.
Put that chair against the wall.

de (of, from, about)
La casa de Conchita
Conchita's house
Estamos hablando de Vd.
We are talking about you.
Trabajo de nueve a dos.
I work from nine to two.

delante de (in front of)
Andaba delante de mí.
He was walking in front of me.

desde (from, more emphatic than **de**)
Desde la ventana se ve el mar.
From the window one can see the sea.

13

después de (after, when referring to time)
Después de cenar daremos un paseo.
After dinner we'll go for a walk.

detrás de (behind)
El garaje está detrás de la casa.
The garage is behind the house.

en (in, on, at)
El regalo está en la caja.
The present is in the box.
La comida está en la mesa.
The food is on the table.
Estarán en casa todo el día.
They will be at home all day.

encima de (on top of, over)
La maleta está encima del armario.
The suitcase is on top of the wardrobe.

enfrente de (opposite)
La farmacia está enfrente del banco.
The drugstore is opposite the bank.

entre (between)
Podemos pagar los gastos entre nosotros.
We can pay the expenses between us.

hacia (towards, about: in reference to time)
El niño vino hacia nosotros.
The boy came toward us.
Volveremos hacia el veinte de septiembre.
We'll come back toward September 20.

hasta (until, as far as)
Durmió hasta las once.
He slept until eleven.
Me acompañó hasta la parada de autobús.
He accompanied me as far as the bus stop.

13

según (according to)
Según la previsión meteorológica, va a llover.
According to the weather forecast, it's going to rain.

sin (without)
No podemos viajar sin pasaporte.
We cannot travel without a passport.

sobre (on, upon, about)
Las cartas están sobre la mesa.
The letters are on the table.
Tenemos que hablar sobre ese tema.
We have to talk about that subject.

tras (after)
El perro corrió tras la pelota.
The dog ran after the ball.

VOCABULARY 3

espléndido	generous (also, magnificent)
la fila	line, row
el juez/la jueza	judge
la cama	bed
la zapatería	shoe store
la panadería	bakery
el piso	floor, story
probar	to try, to test
el sofá	sofa
el paquete	parcel, package
el escritorio	desk

13

Exercise 3

Translate:

1 The man was sleeping under a tree.
2 He wrote to me from Córdoba.
3 After the theater, we went to his house.
4 He is very generous with his friends.
5 We waited at the door, but he did not come.
6 According to his father, he is very ill.
7 There was a long line of cars in front of me.
8 He had to appear before the judge.
9 They left without paying for the drink.
10 He put the suitcase under the bed.
11 There is a shoe store opposite the bakery.
12 I won't see you (fam. sing.) until Sunday.
13 The elevator stopped between the two floors.
14 I want to try it before buying it.
15 We'll start walking toward the station.
16 They will have to go on the bus.
17 The book has fallen behind the sofa.
18 I will leave the parcel on top of the desk.

13.6 AUGMENTATIVES AND DIMINUTIVES

Certain augmentative and diminutive endings can be added to nouns to qualify their meaning. The use of these endings can be tricky, as they can have positive or negative connotations, so it's probably best to avoid using them when referring to people.

1 Augmentatives

-ón, **-azo**, **-acho**, **-ote** express largeness and may also imply some degree of awkwardness or ugliness:

un hombretón a big man
unos ojazos big eyes
una mujerona a big woman

13

2 Diminutives

-ito, **-ico**, **-illo**, **-uelo** express smallness and sometimes fondness on the part of the speaker:

un perrito a little dog
un corrillo a small circle of people
un polluelo a chick

Many augmentatives and diminutives have established themselves as words in their own right:

ventana (window)→ **ventanilla** (window of a vehicle)
silla (chair)→ **sillín** (saddle)**, sillón** (armchair)
puerta (door)→ **portón** (large door, gate)
cera (wax)→ **cerillas** (matches)
caja (box)→ **cajón** (drawer)
camisa (shirt)→ **camisón** (nightgown)
pan (bread)→ **panecillo** (roll)
niebla (fog)→ **neblina** (mist)

13.7 IDIOMATIC USES OF CERTAIN VERBS

The following lists some idiomatic uses and meanings of some common verbs.

1 caer (to fall)

La pobre mujer cayó enferma y murió a las dos semanas.
The poor woman fell ill and died two weeks later.

Es un hombre que me cae mal.
He is a man I dislike.

Ese vestido te cae muy bien.
That dress fits you very well.

No han caído en la cuenta.
They haven't "caught on."

2 dar (to give)

Vamos a dar un paseo. / Vamos a dar una vuelta.
Let's go for a walk.

Las dos hermanas se dieron un abrazo.
The two sisters embraced each other.

Al ver al ladrón, di un grito.
On seeing the burglar, I screamed.

Las ventanas de los dormitorios dan a una pequeña plaza.
The bedroom windows overlook a little square.

No olvides dar de comer al perro.
Don't forget to feed the dog.

No se dio cuenta del error.
He didn't realize the mistake.

No puedo seguir jugando; me doy por vencido.
I can't go on playing, I give up.

Es tarde; tenemos que dar la vuelta.
It's late, we have to turn back.

Voy a darle los buenos días a tu madre.
I'm going to say good morning to your mother.

Tenemos que darnos prisa o no llegaremos a tiempo.
We have to hurry or we won't be on time.

Han ido a dar parte del robo a la policía.
They have gone to report the theft to the police.

Al despedirse, se dieron la mano.
As they said goodbye, they shook hands.

Podemos tomar vino blanco o tinto, lo mismo me da.
We can have white or red wine, it's all the same to me.

3 dejar(se) (to allow, to leave behind)

Sus padres no le dejan salir.
His parents won't let him go out.
Hemos dejado el coche en el aparcamiento.
We have left the car in the parking lot.

Me dejé el paraguas en el taxi.
I left my umbrella in the taxi.

4 dejar de (to give up, to stop)

¿Cuándo vas a dejar de trabajar?
When are you going to stop working?

No dejes de llamarme.
Do call me.

5 despedir(se) (to dismiss, to say goodbye to)

Han despedido a cien empleados.
They have dismissed 100 employees.

Carmen vino a despedirme al aeropuerto.
Carmen came to see me off at the airport.

6 echar (to throw)

Echa estos periódicos a la papelera de reciclaje.
Throw these newspapers in the recycling bin.

Tenemos que echar estas cartas antes de las cuatro.
We have to mail these letters before four o'clock.

No debes echar la culpa a Juan.
You mustn't blame Juan.

Cuando vi el autobús, eché a correr, pero no pude cogerlo.
When I saw the bus, I started to run, but I couldn't catch it.

13

Me gusta vivir en Nueva York, pero echo de menos el clima del Mediterráneo.
I like living in New York, but I miss the Mediterranean climate.

Siempre está dispuesto a echar una mano.
He is always ready to lend a hand.

No olvides echar la llave a la puerta.
Don't forget to lock the door.

7 llevar(se) (to carry, to take, to wear)

Tuvimos que llevarlo al médico.
We had to take him to the doctor.

No me gusta llevar sombrero.
I don't like to wear a hat.

Los dos hermanos se llevan muy bien.
The two brothers get on very well.

Mi marido me lleva cuatro años.
My husband is four years older than I.

No le gusta cuando le llevan la contraria.
He doesn't like it when they contradict him.

Viven en el campo y llevan una vida muy tranquila.
They live in the country and they lead a very quiet life.

8 valer (to be worth, to cost)

¿Cuánto vale el alquiler del coche?
How much is the car rental?

Más vale ir directamente al hotel.
It's better to go straight to the hotel.

No vale la pena esperar.
It's not worth waiting.

13

Drills 1–2

Example:
¿Necesitas el paraguas? Do you need the umbrella?
No, no me hace falta. No, I don't need it.
¿Necesitan (Vds.) sellos? Do you need stamps?
No, no nos hacen falta. No, we don't need them.

1 ¿Necesita Carmen el coche?
2 ¿Necesitáis el pasaporte?
3 ¿Necesita (Vd.) estas cajas?
4 ¿Necesitan ellos ayuda?
5 ¿Necesita Ramón las gafas?
6 ¿Necesitan (Vds.) otra maleta?

Example:
Ha firmado (Vd.) la carta? Have you signed the letter?
No puedo firmarla todavía. I cannot sign it yet.

1 ¿Habéis devuelto el dinero?
2 ¿Has metido la ropa en la maleta?
3 ¿Han echado ellos las postales?
4 ¿Te has quitado los zapatos?
5 ¿Han tomado (Vds.) vino?
6 ¿Ha pagado Carlos la cuenta?

Fill in the blanks with the appropriate preposition from the column on the right.

1 Trabajaré … las cinco.	en
2 Nos escribirá … Sevilla.	sin
3 El hotel está … la playa.	hacia
4 He dejado la maleta … la cama.	antes de
5 … los dos podemos mover el armario.	enfrente de
6 No puedes salir … abrigo.	desde
7 Queremos hablar … el gerente.	encima de
8 No podré llegar … las diez.	con
9 Te esperaremos … casa.	entre
10 Los niños corrieron … su padre.	hasta

13

En el tren

ALBA   Perdone, ¿está ocupado este asiento?

FELIPE   No, no creo.

ALBA   Menos mal. Creí que no iba a encontrar sitio. El tren está casi lleno.

FELIPE   Es verdad. Nunca había visto tanta gente en este tren.

ALBA   ¿Le importa que cierre la cortina? Entra demasiado sol.

FELIPE   No, ciérrela si quiere. A mí también me molesta. ¿Quiere un chicle?

ALBA   ¿De qué sabor es?

FELIPE   Es de fresa.

ALBA   Sí, gracias. Me encantan los chicles de fresa. Bueno, parece que nos ponemos en marcha. ¿Va a Segovia?

FELIPE   Sí. Tengo que visitar una fábrica allí. No voy a estar más que dos días. ¿Y Vd.?

ALBA   Yo también voy a Segovia, a pasar una semana con unos amigos. ¡Ay, qué rabia! He olvidado comprar algo para leer en el viaje.

FELIPE   ¿Quiere esta revista?

ALBA   Si a Vd. no le hace falta de momento, me gustaría verla. Gracias.

13

On the train

ALBA Excuse me. Is this seat taken?

FELIPE No, I don't think so.

ALBA Thank goodness. I thought I wasn't going to find a place. The train is almost full.

FELIPE It's true. I have never seen so many people on this train.

ALBA Do you mind if I close the blind? There's too much sun coming in.

FELIPE No, close it if you want. It's also bothering me. Would you like chewing gum?

ALBA What flavor is it?

FELIPE It's strawberry.

ALBA Yes, thanks. I love strawberry chewing gum.... Well, it looks as if we're moving. Are you going to Segovia?

FELIPE Yes. I have to visit a factory there. I'm only going to stay a couple of days. And you?

ALBA I'm going to Segovia, too, to spend a week with some friends. Oh, how annoying! I forgot to buy something to read on the journey.

FELIPE Would you like this magazine?

ALBA If you don't need it for the moment, I'd like to look at it. Thank you.

13

Review exercises

Exercise 1

Translate:

1 They must have gone out.
2 She could neither read nor write.
3 We ought to wait a few more minutes.
4 Can you (pol. sing.) tell me the time?
5 He was afraid because he could not swim.
6 You (fam. sing.) should invite her to dinner.
7 They owe me twelve euros.
8 You (fam. pl.) must decide what you want to do.

Exercise 2

Put the verbs in brackets into the correct form of the present subjunctive:

1 Quiere que nosotros [ir] con ella.
2 Necesito que él me [ayudar] en la cocina.
3 Es preferible que ellos [quedarse] en casa.
4 Le han prohibido que [salir].
5 No quieren que yo lo [saber].
6 Sentimos que usted no [poder] venir.
7 Es probable que [llover] hoy.
8 Me alegro de que vosotros [tener] éxito.
9 No le gusta que su hija [jugar] con esos niños.
10 No quiero que tú [llegar] tarde.
11 Se lo diremos cuando la [ver].
12 Esperaremos hasta que él [venir].
13 Dígale a Paco que me [llamar].
14 Dudo que ellos [tener] suficiente dinero.
15 No debes permitirle que lo [hacer].
16 ¿Hay alguien que me [acompañar]?

13

Exercise 3

Turn the verbs in brackets in the following phrases into commands using the "tú" form:

1 [Esperar] un momento.
2 [Sentarse] aquí.
3 [Darle] las llaves.
4 [Hacer] el café.
5 No [pedir] más caramelos.
6 [Tener] cuidado.
7 No [traer] al perro.
8 [Venir] pasado mañana.

Exercise 4

Turn the verbs in brackets in the following phrases into commands using the "vosotros" form:

1 [Limpiar] vuestra habitación.
2 No [volver] a casa tarde.
3 [Comer] en la cafetería.
4 [Acostarse] temprano.
5 No [decirle] que estoy enfermo.
6 No [ir] a España en agosto.
7 [Escribir] vuestro nombre aquí.
8 No [telefonearme] antes de las once.

Exercise 5

Put the verbs in brackets into either of the correct forms of the subjunctive:

1 Nos extrañó que él no [estar] allí.
2 Le dije que me lo [enviar] al hotel.
3 Nos pidió que lo [perdonar].
4 No quisieron que yo [ir] al aeropuerto.
5 Te lo diríamos si lo [saber].
6 Ojalá tú [poder] venir de vacaciones conmigo.
7 Era importante que ellas [firmar] ese documento.
8 Podrían comer en el jardín si [hacer] mejor tiempo.
9 Yo no estaría aquí si eso [ser] verdad.
10 Pedro no te daría dinero aunque tú lo [necesitar].
11 Nos aconsejó que no [vender] la casa.
12 Me dijo que [traer] el pasaporte.

Exercise 6

Your friend Paco, whom you haven't seen for some time, calls you to arrange a meeting. Answer him in Spanish.

PACO Te llamo porque hace mucho tiempo que no nos vemos.
USTED I know. I've had a lot of work.
PACO ¿Por qué no vamos a cenar mañana?
USTED I'm sorry. I haven't any free evenings this week.
PACO Entonces, dime cuando podemos vernos.
USTED Saturday of next week?
PACO ¡Vale! ¿Dónde quieres que nos veamos?
USTED Come to my house at 8 p.m. We'll have a drink and then decide where to go for dinner.
PACO ¿No crees que debiéramos reservar una mesa? Todos los restaurantes van a estar llenos.
USTED Perhaps you're right. Do you want me to make a reservation in a restaurant not far from where I live?
PACO Muy bien. Te lo dejo a ti. Nos vemos en tu casa. Adiós. Hasta el sábado.
USTED Goodbye, and thanks for calling.

13

Exercise 7

Complete the following sentences, using the appropriate idiom with the verb "tener" in the correct form:

1 Me voy a bañar en la piscina porque ….
2 No quería quedarse sola en casa porque ….
3 Se puso la chaqueta porque ….
4 Vamos a tomar una cerveza porque ….
5 Se acostaron temprano porque ….
6 No pudimos esperar más porque ….
7 Nos reímos mucho con la película porque ….
8 No tomaron nada para desayunar porque ….
9 No ganaré nunca la lotería porque ….

Exercise 8

Translate:

1 That coat doesn't fit you (fam. sing.) very well.
2 He has fallen ill and has been taken to the hospital.
3 We decided to go for a short walk.
4 Hurry up (fam. sing.)! The train leaves at 9:45.
5 He never says good morning to me.
6 They started to go up the mountain, but they soon gave up.
7 I have come to say goodbye.
8 We can't blame anyone.
9 You (fam. sing.) must miss Pedro, he was a good friend of yours.
10 Did you (pol. sing.) lock the suitcase before leaving the room?
11 I don't want you to contradict me.
12 We get on very well, we never argue.
13 It's better to take the umbrella, it may rain.

13

Exercise 9

Translate:

1 What a lot of people!
2 The man we saw yesterday is her husband.
3 Whose magazines are these?
4 Which seat do you (fam. sing.) prefer?
5 What a boring film!
6 The woman for whom she works is an actress.
7 How difficult it is to see him!
8 The room in which we slept overlooked the sea.
9 Those who need more information may ask that lady.
10 You (fam. sing.) must show me the present he has given you.
11 It is we who have to send it.
12 He didn't want to go, which surprised me.
13 I asked him who had come, but he didn't tell me.
14 That is the woman whose house they have bought.
15 They are friends with whom I am always in touch.
16 What we don't understand is why he hasn't written.

Reading practice

Un tour por Europa

Cuando recibí una invitación para ir a una boda en Verona, Italia, me puse muy contento. ¡Podría coger el tren y hacer un tour por Europa! Así que, una mañana de julio, salí con una mochila, un rail pass y una cartera llena de euros y empecé mi aventura.

Cogí un tren de Londres a Ámsterdam y pasé un fin de semana divertido paseando en bicicleta por los canales y probando deliciosos quesos holandeses. Luego fui a Múnich y visité su enorme parque central, el Englischer Garten. Después, viajé por los Alpes hasta Lyon y luego hasta la costa oeste de Francia. Me llevó varios días, pero el paisaje fue tan espectacular que no me importó. Después de parar en Burdeos para disfrutar de su famoso vino, crucé la frontera para pasar a España y viajé por la costa norte, deteniéndome para probar pintxos en San Sebastián y visitar la catedral en Santiago de Compostela. En Portugal, exploré el encantador casco antiguo de Lisboa en metro, luego volvió a España y visité el Museo del Prado en Madrid y descubrí la extraordinaria arquitectura de Gaudí en Barcelona. Desde allí, volví a Francia y pasé algunos días en los complejos hoteleros de lujo situados al borde del mar de la Costa Azul.

Cuando crucé la frontera italiana y llegué a Génova, supe que mi increíble tour ya estaba a punto de acabar. Pero me quedaba un sitio por visitar: la histórica y romántica ciudad de Verona. La boda fue increíble y disfruté de una de las mejores comidas de mi vida. Fue el final perfecto para un viaje inolvidable.

VOCABULARY

la boda	wedding	**enorme**	huge
salir	set off	**el paisaje**	scenery
la mochila	backpack	**espectacular**	spectacular
el rail pass	rail pass	**no me importó**	didn't mind
divertido/a	enjoyable	**encantador/a**	charming
los canales	canals	**descubrí**	discovered
delicioso/a	delicious	**extraordinario/a**	extraordinary
exploré	explored	**la arquitectura**	architecture

A tour of Europe

When I received an invitation to a wedding in Verona, Italy, I was really excited. I could take the train and go on a tour of Europe! So, one morning in July, I set off with a backpack, a rail pass, and a wallet full of euros and began my adventure!

I took a train from London to Amsterdam and spent an enjoyable weekend cycling along the canals and trying delicious Dutch cheeses. Then I went to Munich and explored its huge central park, the Englischer Garten. Next, I traveled through the Alps to Lyon and then to the west coast of France. It took several days, but the scenery was so spectacular that I didn't mind. After stopping in Bordeaux to enjoy its famous wine, I crossed the border into Spain and traveled along the north coast, stopping to try pinxos in San Sebastián and visit the cathedral in Santiago de Compostela. I explored Lisbon's charming old town by tram, visited the Prado museum in Madrid, and discovered the extraordinary architecture of Gaudí in Barcelona. From there, I returned to France and spent a few days in the stylish seaside resorts of the Côte d'Azur.

When I crossed the Italian border and arrived in Genoa, I knew my amazing tour was almost over. But I had one place left to visit: the historic and romantic city of Verona. The wedding was incredible, and I had one of the best meals of my life. It was the perfect end to an unforgettable trip.

de lujo	stylish
los complejos hoteleros situados al borde del mar	seaside resorts
increíble	incredible
inolvidable	unforgettable

Key to exercises

Week 1

Exercise 1: 1 los libros. 2 las casas. 3 las mujeres. 4 los hombres. 5 las calles. 6 las flores. 7 los jardines. 8 los coches. 9 las capitales. 10 las ciudades. 11 las luces. 12 las leyes.

Exercise 2: 1 los. 2 el. 3 las. 4 la. 5 el. 6 los. 7 el. 8 la. 9 el. 10 las. 11 el. 12 el. (indefinite articles): 1 unos. 2 un. 3 unas. 4 una. 5 un. 6 unos. 7 un. 8 una. 9 un. 10 unas. 11 un. 12 un.

Exercise 3: 1 el libro. 2 la mesa. 3 los billetes. 4 unos árboles. 5 una cerveza. 6 el coche. 7 una ciudad. 8 unas luces. 9 el jardín. 10 una calle. 11 unas mujeres. 12 la estación.

Exercise 4: 1 Tienen una casa. 2 No tenemos café. 3 El hombre tiene miedo. 4 Tengo que trabajar. 5 ¿Tienes un lápiz? 6 No tienen sed. 7 ¿Tienen (Vds.) todo? 8 Tengo calor. 9 Tenemos que salir. 10 Tiene un hijo.

Drill 1: 1 No, no tengo hambre. 2 No, no tenemos cerveza. 3 No, no tengo sed. 4 No, no tenemos calor. 5 No, no tengo frío. 6 No, no tenemos los libros. 7 No, no tenemos los billetes.

WEEK 2

Exercise 1: 1 a la iglesia. 2 del idioma. 3 al coche. 4 a la mesa. 5 de los árboles. 6 a la casa. 7 del hombre. 8 de la ciudad. 9 a la calle. 10 del vino. 11 al policía. 12 de la estación.

Exercise 2: 1 buenos. 2 encantadora. 3 útiles.
4 blancas. 5 barato. 6 larga. 7 altos. 8 interesantes.
9 americano. 10 alemana.

Exercise 3: 1 son. 2 está. 3 son. 4 es. 5 están. 6 está.
7 es. 8 es. 9 está. 10 estoy.

Exercise 4: 1 Es italiana. 2 Las manzanas están en la
cocina. 3 El autobús está allí. 4 Madrid es la capital de
España.
5 La chica es alta. 6 La casa está en la colina.
7 Es peligroso fumar. 8 El café está demasiado dulce.
9 Mañana es domingo. 10 Están en la playa.

WEEK 3

Exercise 1: 1 Ese coche es caro. 2 Esos hombres son
fuertes. 3 Esa iglesia es muy vieja. 4 Estos amigos son
de Málaga. 5 Esta mesa está ocupada. 6 Ese hombre
está libre. 7 Este ascensor está lleno. 8 Esas uvas
están agrias. 9 Aquellos libros son interesantes.
10 Es aquella playa.

Exercise 2: 1 estos, esos. 2 esa, aquella. 3 estas, esas.
4 ese, este. 5 este, aquel. 6 esos, estos. 7 este, ese.
8 ese, este. 9 estas, esas. 10 este, aquel.

Exercise 3: 1 Compro. 2 Sube. 3 (Vd.) bebe.
4 Escribimos. 5 Aprenden. 6 Estudio. 7 Hablas.
8 Come. 9 Vivimos. 10 Suben. 11 Aprendo. 12 Bebe.

Exercise 4: 1 Compra un periódico. 2 ¿Bebe cerveza?
3 Pedro vive en Barcelona. 4 Escribo a Conchita.
5 ¿Estudias inglés? 6 Estos niños aprenden español.

7 Habla demasiado. 8 Subimos la colina. 9 Hablo inglés. 10 Beben vino caro.

Exercise 5: 1 El pueblo en el que vivimos. 2 La mujer que trabaja en la tienda. 3 El libro que tengo que leer. 4 La ciudad de la que estamos hablando. 5 Es María quien es médica. 6 ¿De quién son estas cartas? 7 ¿Qué revista está comprando? 8 La casa que tiene una puerta verde. 9 La pluma con la que escribo. 10 ¿Cuál es el número?

Drill 1: 1 Sí, bebemos cerveza. 2 Sí, como pan. 3 Sí, vivimos en Boston. 4 Sí, soy médico. 5 Sí, hablamos español. 6 Sí, compro la revista.

Drill 2: 1 No, no vivo en Barcelona. 2 No, no comprendo. 3 No, no aprendo alemán. 4 No, no compramos los periódicos. 5 No, no bebo vino. 6 No, no somos españoles.

Drill 3: 1 Está comprando. 2 Están bebiendo. 3 Estoy estudiando. 4 Estamos comiendo. 5 Está leyendo. 6 Estamos hablando. 7 Está escribiendo. 8 Están aprendiendo. 9 Estoy subiendo.

WEEK 4

Exercise 1: 1 mi marido. 2 su hermano. 3 nuestra hermana. 4 su sobrino. 5 su tío. 6 mis padres. 7 tu mujer. 8 sus hijos. 9 su primo. 10 sus parientes.

Exercise 2: 1 la tuya. 2 el suyo. 3 el nuestro. 4 la suya.
5 la nuestra. 6 el mío. 7 la suya. 8 los vuestros.
9 la mía. 10 el suyo.

Exercise 3: 1 diez casas. 2 setenta y dos euros.
3 doscientas mujeres. 4 dieciséis cartas. 5 ciento
treinta y cinco libros. 6 cuarenta y seis hoteles.
7 trescientas cincuenta y cuatro manzanas. 8 sesenta
y ocho tiendas. 9 mil cuatrocientos hombres.
10 setecientos ochenta y cinco coches.

Exercise 4: 1 el séptimo libro. 2 la primera mujer.
3 la tercera hija. 4 el sexto hijo. 5 la segunda puerta.
6 el décimo día. 7 la cuarta calle. 8 el noveno niño.
9 el quinto hombre. 10 la octava tienda.

Exercise 5: 1 ¿Qué hora es? 2 Son las diez y veinte en
mi reloj. 3 Trabajo hasta las once y media. 4 El
invierno en Madrid es frío. 5 Tienen sus vacaciones
en julio. 6 Mi cumpleaños es el tres de enero. 7 Está
libre los sábados. 8 Octubre es generalmente un mes
bonito. 9 Tenemos que ir a Barcelona en mayo.
10 Los domingos ceno con mis padres.

REVIEW EXERCISES

Exercise 1: 1 tengo. 2 viven. 3 es. 4 están. 5 comen.
6 habla. 7 son. 8 cena. 9 aprende. 10 trabajamos.

Exercise 2: 1 En España los periódicos americanos son
muy caros. 2 ¿Dónde están las maletas? 3 La
habitación está en el tercer piso. 4 En el verano viven
en Inglaterra y en el invierno viven en España. 5 Su
marido está ocupado, trabaja demasiado. 6 Tengo que

escribir a mi amiga alemana. 7 Estas flores son para la madre de Juan. 8 La Sra. Suárez es una mujer encantadora. 9 Tenemos que comprar los billetes. 10 ¿Qué hora es? Son las siete y cuarto. 11 ¿Es ese perro suyo? 12 Nuestra hija está aprendiendo español.

Exercise 3: 1 Soy americano/a. 2 No, vivo en Boston. 3 Estoy de vacaciones. 4 Solo dos. 5 Sí, trabajo en una tienda. 6 Es una librería. 7 No, estoy en casa de una amiga. 8 En una casa en la playa. 9 No, gracias, tengo prisa. Adiós.

WEEK 5

Exercise 1: 1 Vamos a la iglesia los domingos. 2 Voy a comprar ese libro. 3 Va a casa de su amigo/a. 4 Vamos de vacaciones en el verano. 5 Van a Madrid en tren. 6 Vamos a tomar un café. 7 No va a cantar. 8 Mañana voy a descansar. 9 Van de compras en el mercado. 10 Vamos al teatro.

Exercise 2: 1 He escrito tres cartas. 2 Han hablado en español. 3 Hemos comido demasiado. 4 Hay azúcar en este té. 5 Ha comprado un vestido nuevo. 6 ¿Has terminado el trabajo? 7 Nunca han ayudado en la casa. 8 Hay unas naranjas en la bolsa. 9 ¿Ha bebido (Vd.) el agua? 10 No he visto la película.

Exercise 3: 1 a. 2 a. 3 –. 4 al. 5 –. 6 a. 7 –. 8 –. 9 –. 10 a.

Exercise 4: 1 Visita a su madre. 2 He visto a la mujer. 3 Tenemos que llamar a los perros. 4 María prepara la comida. 5 Han invitado a sus amigos. 6 Tiene una hermana casada. 7 Voy a comprar un caballo. 8 Tenemos que bañar al niño. 9 Están esperando al profesor. 10 Carlos no ha visto Toledo.

Exercise 5: 1 Juan se lo ofrece. 2 La bebo por la mañana.3 Lo hemos comprado. 4 Me las ha enviado. 5 Se la he escrito. 6 Los comemos. 7 Estos señores no lo comprenden. 8 Tengo que estudiarla. 9 Nos las ha vendido. 10 Se los hemos dado.

Exercise 6: 1 No fume (Vd.). 2 Beba (Vd.) este vino. 3 Envíeme (Vd.) la revista. 4 Léales (Vd.) la carta. 5 Véndale (Vd.) su reloj. 6 Aprenda (Vd.) estos números. 7 Escriba (Vd.) su nombre aquí. 8 No coma (Vd.) esas manzanas. 9 No compre (Vd.) esa carne. 10 No me los dé (Vd.).

Exercise 6 (plurals): 1 No fumen (Vds.). 2 Beban (Vds.) ... 3 Envíenme (Vds.) ... 4 Léanles (Vds.) ... 5 Véndanle (Vds.) 6 Aprendan (Vds.) ... 7 Escriban (Vds.) ... 8 No coman (Vds.) ... 9 No compren (Vds.) ... 10 No me los den (Vds.).

Drill 1: 1 No, voy a tomarla ahora. 2 No, van a ir ahora. 3 No, va a escribirla ahora. 4 No, vamos a hacerlo ahora. 5 No, voy a comprarlos ahora. 6 No, van a verlo ahora. 7 No, vamos a terminarla ahora. 8 No, va a llamarla ahora. 9 No, voy a subirlas ahora. 10 No, vamos a beberlo ahora.

Drill 2: 1 Sí, cómprelo. 2 Sí, súbanlas. 3 Sí, llámelo. 4 Sí, invítenlos. 5 Sí, léala. 6 Sí, envíenlas. 7 Sí, bébala. 8 Sí, véndanla.

Drill 3: 1 Ya lo he preparado. 2 Ya lo hemos llamado. 3 Ya lo he escrito. 4 Ya la hemos tomado. 5 Ya los he comprado. 6 Ya les hemos hablado. 7 Ya los he contado. 8 Ya lo hemos vendido. 9 Ya la he leído.

WEEK 6

Exercise 1: 1 Pedro y Anita se escriben todos los días. 2 El coche va a pararse. 3 Vamos a casarnos. 4 Los niños se acuestan a las ocho. 5 Tenemos que lavarnos. 6 Los dos
hombres se odian. 7 Siempre me pide dinero. 8 Nunca se ayudan. 9 Carlos vuelve de la oficina a las seis y media. 10 Tengo que dormirme. 11 Llévese (Vd.) estas tazas. 12 La calle se llama Baeza. 13 Voy a sentarme aquí. 14 Nos vamos mañana. 15 Me he decidido a vivir en España.

Exercise 2: 1 Estamos trabajando con ellos. 2 Ha comprado un regalo para mí. 3 ¿Va a volver contigo? 4 El tiempo está contra nosotros. 5 Se han ido sin él. 6 Siempre ha vivido conmigo. 7 Estas cartas son para ella. 8 Van a comprar la casa entre ellos. 9 ¿Están los niños contigo? 10 Según él, el viaje es demasiado largo.

Exercise 3: 1 ¿Qué tiempo hace? 2 Hoy hace mucho frío. 3 Va a llover mañana. 4 No me gusta esta cerveza. 5 Va a traernos café. 6 Le gusta salir todas las tardes. 7 No sé dónde está. 8 Van a España porque les gusta el sol. 9 Hace veinticinco años. 10 A Carmen le gusta sentarse en el jardín.

Drill 1: 1 Sí, me gusta mucho. 2 Sí, le gustan mucho. 3 Sí, nos gusta mucho. 4 Sí, nos gusta mucho. 5 Sí, le gusta mucho. 6 Sí, me gustan mucho. 7 Sí, me gusta mucho. 8 Sí, les gusta mucho. 9 Sí, nos gusta mucho. 10 Sí, les gusta mucho.

Drill 2: 1 Sí, trabajo con ella. 2 Sí, es para vosotros. 3 Sí, vuelve conmigo. 4 Sí, vamos sin ellos. 5 Sí, son para ti. 6 Sí, vive con ellos. 7 Sí, son para nosotros. 8 Sí, voy con él.

Drill 3: 1 Sí, quisiera sentarme. 2 Sí, quisiera lavarme. 3 Sí, quisiera dormirme. 4 Sí, quisiera irme. 5 Sí, quisiera pararme. 6 Sí, quisiéramos sentarnos. 7 Sí, quisiéramos lavarnos. 8 Sí, quisiéramos dormirnos. 9 Sí, quisiéramos irnos. 10 Sí, quisiéramos pararnos.

WEEK 7

Exercise 1: 1 Luis vendía un coche. 2 Suelo verla por la mañana. 3 Habían hablado con el gerente del hotel. 4 Solía traerme bombones. 5 El muchacho buscaba su maleta. 6 La función solía empezar a las diez. 7 Había trabajado en una fábrica. 8 El mar estaba muy frío. 9 La mujer nos miraba. 10 Solíamos comer mucho pescado.

Exercise 2: 1 nada. 2 nadie. 3 ni, ni. 4 nunca. 5 ningún. 6 tampoco. 7 nadie. 8 nada. 9 ninguna. 10 nunca.

Exercise 3: 1 felizmente. 2 verdaderamente. 3 tristemente. 4 lentamente. 5 nuevamente. 6 agradablemente. 7 malamente. 8 ciertamente. 9 rápidamente. 10 claramente.

Exercise 4: 1 Mi hermano es más fuerte que yo. 2 Este jerez es más seco que ese. 3 Carlos es tres años mayor que María. 4 Los zapatos negros son más pequeños que los azules. 5 Su coche es mejor que el mío. 6 Escribe peor que su hermana. 7 He llegado más pronto que mi padre. 8 No tienen tanto dinero como sus amigos. 9 No necesito tantas maletas como tú. 10 El agua en la piscina está más caliente que en el mar.

Drill 1: 1 Sí, solía verla. 2 Sí, solían comer. 3 Sí, solíamos trabajar. 4 Sí, solía escribirlas. 5 Sí, solía viajar. 6 Sí, solíamos ir. 7 Sí, solía hablarlo. 8 Sí, solía invitarlos. 9 Sí, solían tenerlo. 10 Sí, solía beberlo.

Drill 2: 1 No, no quiero nada. 2 No, no han vivido aquí nunca. 3 No, no queremos ni té ni café. 4 No, no hay ningún turista inglés. 5 No, no conocemos a nadie. 6 No, no tengo ninguna revista española.

Drill 3: 1 Los míos son más viejos. 2 El mío es peor. 3 El mío es más bonito. 4 El mío es mejor. 5 El mío es más alto. 6 Los míos son más caros. 7 Las mías son más grandes. 8 Los míos son más baratos.

REVIEW EXERCISES

Drill 1: 1 Nos gusta más el vino. 2 Nos gusta más la carne. 3 Le gusta más la playa. 4 Me gusta más el rugby. 5 Les gusta más jugar. 6 Me gusta más Barcelona.

Exercise 1: 1 Voy a una fiesta mañana y necesito un vestido nuevo. 2 Hemos visto una película muy buena en el Roxy. 3 No puede venir a la playa con nosotros, tiene demasiado trabajo. 4 Pedro es muy simpático, pero no tiene paciencia con los niños. 5 La función no empieza hasta las diez y cuarto; es demasiado tarde para nosotros. 6 No han podido salir porque ha llovido todo el día. 7 Tenemos que esperar hasta las cuatro y media porque las tiendas están cerradas.

Drill 2: 1 Sí, lávelo. 2 No, no la espere. 3 Sí, pregúntele. 4 No, no se las lleve. 5 Sí, llámelo. 6 No, no lo invite. 7 Sí, póngalas. 8 No, no lo haga.

Drill 3: 1 Sí, termínenlo. 2 No, no lo pidan. 3 Sí, véanla. 4 No, no se bañen. 5 Sí, cómprenlos. 6 No, no la preparen. 7 Sí, envíenlas. 8 Sí, ayúdenlo.

Exercise 2: 1 (d). 2 (g). 3 (f). 4 (h). 5 (c). 6 (a). 7 (e). 8 (b).

Exercise 3: • Pasado mañana es el cumpleaños de Luisa. •¿Qué podemos comprarle? • Sólo puedo pensar en bombones, flores … • Lee mucho y le gusta viajar. ¿Por qué no le compramos un libro de viajes? • Entonces, vamos de compras esta tarde y buscamos algo.

WEEK 8

Exercise 1: 1 Hemos tenido un buen viaje. 2 Cada hombre tenía un trabajo. 3 Es una gran pintora. 4 Siempre llevan la misma ropa. 5 Hay bastantes hoteles en esta zona. 6 La pobre mujer ha perdido su bolsa. 7 Tengo un sombrero nuevo. 8 Hemos pedido otra bebida. 9 Estos sellos son muy viejos. 10 Todos los niños son buenos nadadores.

Exercise 2: 1 Se casarán el próximo mes. 2 Me acostaré temprano esta noche. 3 Vendrá con nosotros de vacaciones. 4 Los visitaremos el domingo. 5 No quieren hablar con nosotros. 6 Sería mejor parar. 7 No me gustaría conducir un coche grande. 8 No tendrá que andar muy lejos. 9 No valdrían nada. 10 No podremos ver el museo. 11 No quería vender la casa. 12 El autocar saldrá a las ocho.

Exercise 3: 1 Cerraré las ventanas antes de acostarse. 2 Tendré que pensar antes de decidir. 3 No puedes irte antes de terminar el trabajo. 4 Ha pasado el día sin hablar con nadie. 5 Lloraba sin saber por qué. 6 Se sentían enfermos después de comer marisco. 7 Tenía mucho sueño después de trabajar toda la noche. 8 Nos gustaría ver la habitación antes de tomarla. 9 Su voz estaba ronca de gritar tanto. 10 Después de escribir la carta, enséñemela (Vd.).

Drill 1: 1 No, lo verán luego. 2 No, lo terminaremos luego. 3 No, iré luego. 4 No, la escribirá luego. 5 No, las enviaremos luego. 6 No, la cerrarán luego. 7 No, saldrá luego. 8 No, la haré luego. 9 No, las verán luego. 10 No, las abriré luego.

Drill 2: 1 Hace seis meses que estudio español. 2 Hace tres años que estamos en Madrid. 3 Hace dos semanas que trabajan aquí. 4 Hace un año que vive en Los Ángeles. 5 Hace diez minutos que espero. 6 Llevo seis meses estudiando español. 7 Llevamos tres años en Madrid. 8 Llevan dos semanas trabajando aquí. 9 Lleva un año viviendo en Los Ángeles. 10 Llevo diez minutos esperando.

WEEK 9

Exercise 1: 1 Dimos un paseo por el río. 2 No quisieron verme. 3 Puse la carta en el sobre. 4 Murió dos años después. 5 Pagó la comida con tarjeta de crédito. 6 El camarero nos trajo las bebidas y se fue. 7 Anduvieron cinco kilómetros buscando un garaje. 8 Salí a las diez y volví a la hora de comer. 9 Le dijimos que su padre había llegado. 10 No hizo nada toda la mañana.

Exercise 2: 1 salió. 2 estaba, sonó. 3 viajaban, tuvieron. 4 jugaban, empezó. 5 bajó, hacía. 6 se sentaba. 7 volví. 8 hacía, llegamos. 9 recibió, vivía. 10 preguntó.

Exercise 3: 1 No conocen esta película. 2 Sabe que quiero un ordenador portátil. 3 Ese programa de televisión es divertidísimo. 4 Esta talla es la más pequeña que tenemos. 5 Estos zapatos son los más bonitos, esos son los más baratos. 6 Es el hombre más amable que conozco. 7 No saben que deseo verlos. 8 Fue una conversación interesantísima. 9 Es la iglesia más vieja de esta ciudad. 10 La farmacia estaba lejos de la parada de autobús.

Exercise 4: 1 El té es una bebida muy agradable. 2 La señora Collado llegará el domingo. 3 Se puso los guantes porque hacía frío. 4 Él es camarero y ella es dependienta. 5 Pasé dos semanas en el hospital. 6 Lo importante es no preocuparse. 7 La pobre María se ha roto el brazo derecho. 8 Los libros son muy caros hoy día. 9 Andaba con gran dificultad. 10 Va a traer otra taza. 11 Bebimos media botella de zumo. 12 Lo mejor es vender la casa.

Drill 1: 1 pero tuvo que escribirla. 2 pero tuvieron que pagarla. 3 pero tuve que verlo. 4 pero tuvimos que ir. 5 pero tuvo que salir. 6 pero tuvo que hacerla. 7 pero tuvo que comerlo. 8 pero tuvo que ponérselo. 9 pero tuve que dárselo. 10 pero tuvimos que beberlo.

Drill 2: 1 No, estuvimos ayer. 2 No, vinieron ayer. 3 No, lo compré ayer. 4 No, la pagaron ayer. 5 No, la recibió ayer. 6 No, las hicimos ayer. 7 No, llovió ayer. 8 No, las trajeron ayer. 9 No, fuimos ayer. 10 No, los visité ayer.

Drill 3: 1 Sí, es el más bonito que he visto. 2 Sí, son los más caros que he visto. 3 Sí, es la más grande que he visto. 4 Sí, es el más elegante que he visto. 5 Sí, son los más divertidos que he visto. 6 Sí, son las más pequeñas que he visto.

WEEK 10

Exercise 1: 1 por. 2 por. 3 para. 4 por. 5 para. 6 para. 7 por. 8 para. 9 para. 10 por.

Exercise 2: 1 Tenemos que pasar por la Aduana. 2 Nos cobraron veinte euros por la comida. 3 Es demasiado tarde para ir al cine. 4 Necesito una bolsa para todas mis compras. 5 ¿Tiene (Vd.) una llave para abrir este armario? 6 Este libro es demasiado difícil para él. 7 El avión sale para Madrid a las siete y cuarto. 8 Haría cualquier cosa por él. 9 Leímos la carta por curiosidad. 10 Quiere comprar unos melocotones para su madre.

Exercise 3: 1 La casa fue construida por su abuelo.
2 Fui acusado del robo. 3 El barco se vendió por
quinientos euros. 4 El trabajo está terminado ahora.
5 Se cree que está muerto. 6 Las montañas estaban
cubiertas de nieve. 7 La cena no se sirve hasta las
nueve. 8 Las ventanas se pintaron hace tres semanas.
9 Fueron recibidos por uno de los directores.
10 El programa fue presentado por un famoso actor.

Exercise 4: 1 Jugué con los niños toda la tarde.
2 Están construyendo un aparcamiento nuevo.
3 Oyó un ruido arriba. 4 Me sequé los pies al fuego.
5 Cayeron al suelo. 6 Está leyendo las instrucciones.
7 Huyeron de España al principio de la guerra.
8 Pagué mucho dinero por ese cuadro. 9 Coja (Vd.) el
equipaje, por favor. 10 Creyó que la tienda estaba
cerrada.

Exercise 5: 1 Conseguí hablar con ellos. 2 Nos
aconsejó alquilar un coche. 3 Intentaron entrar en la
habitación. 4 Pienso quejarme del servicio. 5 Estamos
aprendiendo a jugar al tenis. 6 Volví a telefonear. 7 El
señor Solís acaba de llegar. 8 Se cansó de subir y se
sentó. 9 Dejó de llover y salió el sol. 10 Me olvidé de
darle el recado. 11 Insistieron en pagar sus billetes.
12 El paquete tardó dos semanas en llegar.
13 Acabaron por tener una discusión. 14 La mujer se
esforzó por sonreír. 15 El hombre amenazó con
llamar a la policía. 16 Se contenta con ganar
muy poco.

Drill 1: 1 para. 2 por. 3 para. 4 para. 5 por. 6 para.
7 para. 8 por.

Drill 2: 1 El libro se publicó. 2 Los coches se alquilaron. 3 La puerta se abrió. 4 Los ruidos se oyeron. 5 El trabajo se terminó. 6 La casa se construyó. 7 Los barcos se vendieron. 8 La carta se leyó.

Drill 3: 1 Sí, acabo de comprarlos. 2 Sí, acaban de llegar. 3 Sí, acabo de recibirlas. 4 Sí, acabamos de hacerlas. 5 Sí, acaban de acostarse. 6 Sí, acabo de encontrarla.

REVIEW EXERCISES

Exercise 1: 1 iremos. 2 cuidará. 3 trabajaré. 4 se levantará. 5 saldremos. 6 vendrá. 7 hará. 8 dará. 9 podrán. 10 tendrás.

Exercise 2: 1 traería. 2 volverían. 3 viajaría. 4 pagarían. 5 enviaría. 6 tendrían.

Exercise 3: 1 Anoche vi a Antonio con su mujer. 2 El tren llegó dos horas tarde. 3 Ofreció ayudarme con las bolsas. 4 No necesitamos ninguna ropa de invierno. 5 Vendieron la casa a un amigo suyo. 6 Conduje cien kilómetros sin parar. 7 Fue a buscar una farmacia. 8 No le gustó el libro que le di.

Exercise 4: • Muy bien. Fue un viaje muy interesante. • Fuimos a Córdoba, Granada y Sevilla. • Mi mujer había estado en Sevilla, pero yo no conocía ninguna de ellas. • No sé. Es difícil elegir una. Cada una tiene una belleza diferente. Posiblemente Granada. La Alhambra es maravillosa. • Alberto, me gustaría seguir hablando, pero tengo que ir de compras con mi mujer. Estará esperándome. Te llamaré el viernes.

Exercise 5: 1 ¿Por qué necesitas dinero? 2 Lo necesito para comprar un coche nuevo. 3 Salieron ayer para Argentina. 4 Estoy haciendo esto por ti. 5 Estamos demasiado cansados para andar a la estación. 6 El hotel cuesta cinquenta euros por persona. 7 Me ha invitado a su casa por un mes. 8 Me enviaron una postal para decirme que venían.

Exercise 6: 1 Se han cancelado los vuelos. 2 Lo acompañó su mujer. 3 Se ha censurado la película. 4 Se anunciaron las elecciones en octubre. 5 La policía arrestó al muchacho. 6 El rey inauguró la exposición. 7 La explosión se oyó en todo el pueblo. 8 El banco no ha aceptado el cheque.

Exercise 7: 1 de, a. 2 a. 3 –. 4 a, de. 5 en. 6 a. 7 a. 8 –. 9 –. 10 de. 11 en. 12 –. 13 a. 14 –. 15 de. 16 con.

Exercise 8: 1 Todos estamos cansados hoy. 2 Mi hija quiere ser abogada. 3 Cuando estuvo enfermo, yo iba a visitarlo todos los días. 4 No te sientes en esa silla, está rota. 5 Hace mucho calor, aunque todas las ventanas están abiertas. 6 Está triste porque su mejor amigo se ha muerto. 7 Siempre estoy en casa los domingos. 8 Es una mujer muy inteligente, pero no muy amable. 9 ¿Quién es (usted)? Soy un amigo suyo. 10 Estábamos para salir cuando él llegó. 11 No le dieron el trabajo porque era demasiado joven. 12 Estas no son mis maletas, las mías son negras.

Exercise 9: 1 íbamos, nos quedábamos. 2 hizo, pidió. 3 tenía, podía. 4 llamó, estaba. 5 llevábamos, llegó. 6 fueron, volvieron, hacía. 7 llegué, estaba. 8 dejó, di. 9 salió, había. 10 trabajó, estaba.

Exercise 1: 1 ¿Cuánto le debo? 2 No deberían decir esas cosas. 3 Debe de tener un buen trabajo. 4 Debo ver a un médico. 5 ¿Sabe hablar español? 6 No puedo leer sin gafas. 7 Deberíamos ir allí más a menudo. 8 Me debe una explicación. 9 Ese anillo debe de costar mucho dinero. 10 No sé montar en bicicleta. 11 No puede tomar una pastilla sin agua. 12 ¿Sabes cocinar?

Exercise 2: 1 Me alegro de que puedan venir. 2 Quiere que el abogado vea los documentos. 3 Nos han mandado que esperemos aquí. 4 Dudo que salga el sol. 5 Me sorprende que no haya escrito. 6 Me ha pedido que le enseñe español. 7 Es posible que se hayan perdido. 8 Es una lástima que no tengamos bastante dinero. 9 Es probable que se casen. 10 No podré hacerlo a no ser que me ayuden. 11 Iremos al cine con tal que me dejes pagar. 12 Esperará hasta que yo vuelva. 13 Tendrán que comerlo, aunque no les guste. 14 No hay nadie que pueda pagar ese precio. 15 ¿Hay alguien que sepa tocar el piano? 16 Necesito alguien que cuide de los niños. 17 Lo encontraremos, dondequiera que esté. 18 Te ayudará cuandoquiera que tengas un problema. 19 Por mucho que trate, nunca tendrá éxito. 20 Por muy fácil que parezca, se necesita práctica.

Exercise 3: 1 Hazlo. No lo hagas. 2 Ven. No vengas. 3 Acuéstate. No te acuestes. 4 Aprende. No aprendas. 5 Ponlo. No lo pongas. 6 Escríbela. No la escribas. 7 Grita. No grites. 8 Óyelo. No lo oigas. 9 Preocúpate. No te preocupes. 10 Duérmete. No te duermas.

Exercise 4: 1 No te enfades. 2 Escuchadme. 3 Vístete. 4 No me digáis eso. 5 Tened cuidado. 6 Léenoslo. 7 Callaos. 8 No me despiertes temprano. 9 Perdonad mi error. 10 No muevas el coche.

Drill 1: 1 Sí, debe de estar enfermo. 2 Sí, deben de ser las cinco. 3 Sí, deben de estar muy tristes. 4 Sí, debe de trabajar mucho. 5 Sí, debe de hacer muchos años. 6 Sí, deben de estar en casa.

Drill 2: 1 Sí, es preferible que coman. 2 Sí, es preferible que se vaya. 3 Sí, es preferible que volvamos. 4 Sí, es preferible que se acuesten. 5 Sí, es preferible que pague. 6 Sí, es preferible que nos sentemos.

Drill 3: 1 Sí, pedidlos. 2 Sí, tráelo. 3 Sí, llamadlo. 4 Sí, cómpralo. 5 Sí, abridlas. 6 Sí, ayúdalo.

Drill 4: 1 No, siguen comiendo. 2 No, sigue leyéndolo. 3 No, seguimos trabajando. 4 No, sigo pintando. 5 No, sigue cantando. 6 No, siguen construyéndola.

WEEK 12

Exercise 1: 1 Querían que viajase con ellos. 2 Tenía miedo de que hubiera tenido un accidente. 3 Nos dijo que pusiéramos la mesa. 4 Le pedí que se diera prisa. 5 Esperábamos que no hiciese demasiado calor en Sevilla. 6 Dondequiera que fuese, siempre encontraba amigos. 7 Lo avisé para no usara esa máquina. 8 Me llamó por teléfono para que reservara las habitaciones. 9 Buscaban a una persona que pudiese traducir la carta. 10 Me alegro de que ganaran el primer premio.

Exercise 2: 1 Lo haría si pudiera. 2 Si hace buen tiempo, trabajaré en el jardín. 3 El perro no te habría mordido si no lo hubieses asustado. 4 Si les preguntaras, no sabrían que decir. 5 Si lo viera ahora, no le hablaría. 6 (Vd.) no habría perdido el dinero si lo hubiera guardado en su bolsillo. 7 Si vinieran a la fiesta, se divertirían. 8 Te escribiré si tengo que quedarme allí más tiempo. 9 Si no llevas paraguas, te mojarás. 10 Yo iría al concierto si él viniera conmigo.

Exercise 3: 1 Ojalá no tuviera que trabajar. 2 Quizá esté enfermo. 3 Puede que haya perdido el tren. 4 Que venga si quiere. 5 Ojalá pudiéramos tener unas vacaciones. 6 Pase lo que pase, estaré en contacto con Vd(s). 7 ¿Podemos ver las fotografías? 8 Dijo que yo podía tener el día libre. 9 ¡Que te diviertas! 10 Quizá no vieran el aviso.

Exercise 4: 1 No te acerques al borde. 2 Se asomó a la ventanilla del coche. 3 Mi hermano va a casarse con una inglesa. 4 Sabes que puedes contar conmigo. 5 La ventana daba a una calle muy concurrida. 6 El éxito de la obra depende de los actores. 7 Tengo que despedirme de mis compañeros. 8 No dudan de su buena intención. 9 María se ha enamorado de un hombre muy tonto. 10 Es muy fácil encontrarse con turistas americanas en España. 11 No hemos podido enterarnos de su nombre. 12 No me fijé en lo que llevaba. 13 Tienes que ocuparte de las bebidas. 14 Esta casa se parece mucho a la nuestra. 15 No quiere pensar en todos los problemas. 16 No sabemos lo que piensa de la situación. 17 Este helado sabe a fresa. 18 Soñaba con todos los lugares que había visitado.

Drill 1: 1 Puede que lo venda. 2 Puede que se casen. 3 Puede que salgamos. 4 Puede que vuelva. 5 Puede que nos inviten. 6 Puede que nade.

Drill 2: 1 Vendrían si pudieran. 2 Lo pediríamos si lo necesitáramos. 3 Comería si tuviera hambre. 4 Se lo diríamos si lo viéramos. 5 Saldrían si no lloviera. 6 Te lo daría si lo encontrara. 7 Trabajaría más si le pagaran bien. 8 Hablaría con ellos si vinieran.

Drill 3: 1 Se sorprendió al oír la noticia. 2 Gritaron al ver a los policías. 3 Lloraba al leer la carta. 4 Me pidió la llave al salir. 5 Tuve miedo al oír un ruido. 6 Se lavaron las manos al terminar. 7 Me quité el sombrero al entrar. 8 Empezó a llover al llegar a casa.

WEEK 13

Exercise 1: 1 Mucha gente asistió al entierro. 2 Esta cantidad de harina bastará. 3 Esa caja no cabe en el maletero. 4 Quiero devolver la revista que me prestó. 5 Echó la pelota a los niños. 6 Voy a echar el vino. 7 Les falta experiencia. 8 Faltan cinco libros de este estante. 9 Nos hacen falta más ayudantes. 10 Meterán toda la ropa en una maleta. 11 ¿Cuántos días te quedan? 12 Quitará estas sillas. 13 ¿Puedo quitarme la chaqueta? 14 Sobran huevos para hacer la tortilla. 15 Es muy agradable tocar seda. 16 Le gustaría tocar el violín. 17 Tomó la pluma y firmó la carta. 18 Les gusta tomar vino con su comida.

Exercise 2: 1 Ha heredado más de un millón de euros. 2 No puedo venderlo por menos de cien euros. 3 Hemos vivido en Madrid más de quince años. 4 Lo haré en menos de cinco minutos. 5 Nunca había

visto un collar tan bonito. 6 ¡Qué edificio tan feo!
7 No haría tal cosa. 8 Encuentro tales libros muy
aburridos. 9 Ese no es mi hermano, sino mi primo.
10 No tienen un perro, pero tienen dos gatos.
11 Tiene más dinero de lo que dice. 12 Son más listos
de lo que crees. 13 ¡Qué idea tan buena!
14 ¡Es un viaje tan largo!

Exercise 3: 1 El hombre dormía bajo un árbol. 2 Me
escribió desde Córdoba. 3 Después del teatro, fuimos
a su casa. 4 Es muy espléndido con sus amigos.
5 Esperamos a la puerta, pero no vino. 6 Según su
padre, está muy enfermo. 7 Había un fila larga de
coches delante de mí. 8 Tuvo que presentarse ante el
juez. 9 Se fueron sin pagar la bebida. 10 Puso la
maleta debajo de la cama. 11 Hay una zapatería
enfrente de la panadería. 12 No te veré hasta el
domingo. 13 El ascensor se paró entre los dos pisos.
14 Quiero probarlo antes de comprarlo.
15 Empezaremos a andar hacia la estación.
16 Tendrán que ir en el autobús. 17 El libro ha
caído detrás del sofá. 18 Dejaré el paquete encima
del escritorio.

Drill 1: 1 No, no le hace falta. 2 No, no nos hace falta.
3 No, no me hacen falta. 4 No, no les hace falta.
5 No, no le hacen falta. 6 No, no nos hace falta.

Drill 2: 1 No podemos devolverlo todavía. 2 No puedo
meterla ... 3 No pueden echarlas ... 4 No puedo
quitármelos ... 5 No podemos tomarlo ... 6 No puede
pagarla ...

Drill 3: 1 hasta. 2 desde. 3 enfrente de. 4 encima de.
5 entre. 6 sin. 7 con. 8 antes de. 9 en. 10 hacia.

REVIEW EXERCISES

Exercise 1: 1 Deben de haber salido. 2 No sabía ni leer ni escribir. 3 Deberíamos esperar unos minutos más. 4 ¿Puede (usted) decirme la hora? 5 Tenía miedo porque no sabía nadar. 6 Deberías invitarla a cenar. 7 Me deben doce euros. 8 Debéis decidir lo que queréis hacer.

Exercise 2: 1 vayamos. 6 ayude. 3 se queden. 4 salga. 5 sepa. 6 pueda. 7 llueva. 8 tengáis. 9 juegue. 10 llegues. 11 veamos. 12 venga. 13 llame. 14 tengan. 15 haga. 16 acompañe.

Exercise 3: 1 Espera ... 2 Siéntate ... 3 Dale ... 4 Haz ... 5 No pidas ... 6 Ten ... 7 No traigas ... 8 Ven ...

Exercise 4: 1 Limpiad. 2 No volváis. 3 Comed. 4 Acostaos. 5 No le digáis. 6 No vayáis. 7 Escribíd. 8 No me telefoneéis.

Exercise 5: 1 estuviera / estuviese. 2 enviara / enviase. 3 perdonáramos / perdonásemos. 4 fuera / fuese. 5 supiéramos / supiésemos. 6 pudieras / pudieses. 7 firmaran / firmasen. 8 hiciera / hiciese. 9 fuera / fuese. 10 necesitaras / necesitases. 11 vendiéramos / vendiésemos. 12 trajera / trajese.

Exercise 6: • Ya lo sé. He tenido mucho trabajo. • Lo siento. No tengo ninguna noche libre esta semana. • ¿El sábado de la semana próxima? • Ven a mi casa a las ocho. Tomaremos un aperitivo y luego decidiremos adónde ir a cenar. • Quizás tengas razón. ¿Quieres que haga una reserva en un restaurante no lejos de donde vivo? • Adiós y gracias por llamar.

Exercise 7: 1 tengo calor. 2 tenía miedo. 3 tenía frío. 4 tenemos sed. 5 tenían sueño. 6 teníamos prisa. 7 tenía gracia. 8 no tenían hambre. 9 no tengo suerte.

Exercise 8: 1 Ese abrigo no te cae muy bien. 2 Ha caído enfermo y lo han llevado al hospital. 3 Decidimos dar un paseo corto. 4 ¡Date prisa! El tren sale a las diez menos cuarto. 5 Nunca me da los buenos días. 6 Empezaron a subir la montaña, pero pronto se dieron por vencidos. 7 He venido a despedirme. 8 No podemos echar la culpa a nadie. 9 Debes de echar de menos a Pedro; era un buen amigo tuyo. 10 ¿Echó usted la llave a la maleta antes de salir de la habitación? 11 No quiero que me lleves la contraria. 12 Nos llevamos muy bien, nunca discutimos. 13 Más vale llevar el paraguas. Es posible que llueva.

Exercise 9: 1 ¡Cuánta gente! 2 El hombre que vimos ayer es su marido. 3 ¿De quién son estas revistas? 4 ¿Qué asiento prefieres? 5 ¡Qué película tan aburrida! 6 La mujer para quien trabaja es actriz. 7 ¡Qué difícil es verlo! 8 La habitación en la que dormimos daba al mar. 9 Los que necesiten más información pueden preguntar a esa señora. 10 Tienes que enseñarme el regalo que te ha dado. 11 Somos nosotros quienes tenemos que enviarlo. 12 No quiso ir, lo cual me sorprendió. 13 Le pregunté quién había venido, pero no me lo dijo. 14 Esa es la mujer cuya casa han comprado. 15 Son amigos con quienes siempre estoy en contacto. 16 Lo que no comprendemos es por qué no ha escrito.

Mini-dictionary

The translations given are those found in the course; for alternative meanings, check a full dictionary. In the Spanish–English section, the article indicates the noun's gender. Adjectives are given in the masculine singular, followed by the endings for the feminine and plural. Remember that **CH**, **LL**, and **Ñ** are separate letters in Spanish and are listed separately in the dictionary. Thus **mañana** is found after **manzana**.

SPANISH–ENGLISH

a at, to, in …
(el/la) abogado/a lawyer
(el) abrigo coat
abril April
abrir to open
aburrido (-a/-os/-as) boring
(el/la) abuelo/a grandfather/ grandmother
acabar to finish
acaso perhaps
(el) accidente accident
aceptar to accept
acercarse to approach
acompañar to accompany
aconsejar to advise
acordarse (de) to remember
acostarse to go to bed
(el) actor actor
(la) actriz actress
acusar to accuse
adiós goodbye
adonde where to
(la) Aduana Customs
(el) aeropuerto airport
(la) agencia agency
agosto August
agradable pleasant
agrio (-a/-os/-as) sour
(el) agua water
ahora now
ahorrar to save (money/time)
alegrarse to be glad
alemán (alemana/-es/-as) German
algo something
alguien someone, somebody
alguno (-a/-os/-as) some, any

alquilar to hire, to rent
alto (-a/-os/-as) tall
(el/la) alumno/a student, learner
allí there
amable kind
amanecer to dawn
amenazar to threaten
a menudo often
(el/la) amigo/a friend
andar to walk
(el) anillo ring
anochecer to get dark
ante before
antes de before
anunciar to announce
(el) año year
(el) aparcamiento parking lot
(el) aperitivo aperitif, drink
aprender to learn
apresar to seize
aquel (-la/-los/-las) that/those (over there)
(el) armario cupboard, wardrobe
(el) árbol tree
(el/la) arquitecto/a architect
arrancar to start (a car)
arrestar to arrest
arriba upstairs
(el) ascensor elevator
así (que) thus, so
(el) asiento seat
asistir to assist, to attend
asomarse to lean out
asustar to scare
(el) atasco traffic jam
(el) autobús bus

(el) autocar coach
(el) automóvil car
(el) avión airplane
avisar to warn
(el) aviso warning (sign)
(el/la) ayudante helper
ayudar(se) to help (each other)
(el) azúcar sugar
azul blue

bailar to dance
(el) baile dance, dancing
bajar to go down
bajo under
(la) bala bullet
(el) banco bank
bañar to give someone a bath
bañarse to bathe (oneself)
(el) baño bathroom
barato (-a/-os/-as) cheap
(la) barca rowboat
(el) barco boat, ship
bastante enough, fairly
bastar to suffice, to be enough
beber to drink
(la) bebida drink
(la) bicicleta bicycle
bien well
(el) billete ticket, bill (money)
(el) bocadillo sandwich
(la) boda wedding
(la) bolsa bag
(el) bolsillo pocket
(el) bolso handbag
blanco (-a/-os/-as) white
(los) bombones chocolates
bonito (-a/-os/-as) pretty
(el) borde edge
(la) botella bottle
(el) brazo arm
(la) buena intención goodwill
bueno (-a/-os/-as) good
buscar to look for

(el) caballo horse
caber to fit in/into

cada each
(el) café coffee
(la) caja box
(el) cajón drawer
caliente hot, warm
(el) calor heat
callarse to be quiet
(la) calle street
(la) cama bed
(el/la) camarero/a
  waiter/waitress
(el) cambio change
(el) camino way, road
(el) camión truck
(la) camisa shirt
(el) camisón nightgown
(el) campo country(side)
cancelar to cancel
cansado (-a/-os/-as) tired
cansarse to get tired
cantar to sing
(la) cantidad amount
(la) capital capital
(la) carne meat
(la) carnicería butcher's shop
caro (-a/-os/-as) expensive
(la) carretera road
(la) carta letter
(la) casa house, home
casado (-a/-os/-as) married
casarse to get married
casi almost
castigar to punish
(la) casualidad coincidence
(la) catedral cathedral
celebrar to celebrate
(la) cena dinner
cenar to have dinner
censurar to censor
cerca near
(las) cerillas matches
cerrar to close
(la) cerveza beer
ciego (-a/-os/-as) blind
cierto (-a/-os/-as) certain
(el) cigarrillo cigarette

(el) **cine** cinema
(la) **ciudad** city, town
claro of course (lit, "clear")
(el/la) **cliente/a** client
(el) **clima** climate
cobrar to charge
(el) **coche** car
(la) **cocina** kitchen
cocinar to cook
(el) **colegio** school
(la) **colina** hill
(el) **color** color
(el) **collar** necklace
(el) **comedor** dining room
comer to eat
(la) **comida** meal, food
como how, as, like
(el/la) **compañero/a** colleague,
  companion
(la) **compañía de seguros**
  insurance company
comprar to buy
(las) **compras** purchases, shopping
comprender to understand
comprenderse to understand
  each other
con with
(el) **concierto** concert
concurrido (-a/-os/-as) busy,
  crowded
conducir to drive
conocer to know (of)
conseguir to obtain, to manage
consentir to consent
conservador/a conservative
construir to build
(el/la) **contable** accountant
(el) **contacto** contact
contar to count
contentarse to be satisfied
contento (-a/-os/-as) happy, pleased
contestar to answer
contra against
(la) **conversación** conversation
(el) **coñac** brandy
(la) **corbata** necktie
correcto (-a/-os/-as) correct, right

(el) **correo** mail
(la) **cosa** thing
(la) **costa** coast
costar to cost
(la) **costumbre** custom, habit
creer to believe
(el) **cuadro** painting, picture
cual which
cualquier cosa anything
cuando when
cuanto how much
(el) **cuarto** room, fourth, quarter
cubierto (-a/-os/-as) covered
(la) **cuenta** bill
cuidar to look after
(la) **culpa** blame, fault
(el) **cumpleaños** birthday
(la) **curiosidad** curiosity
(la) **chaqueta** jacket
(el) **cheque** check
(el/la) **chico/a** boy/girl

(el) **daño** damage, injury
dar to give
darse prisa to hurry
dar un paseo to go for a walk
de of, from
debajo (de) under, underneath
deber must, should, to owe
decidir to decide
decidirse a to decide
décimo (-a/-os/-as) tenth
decir to say
dejar(se) to let, to allow, to leave
  behind
delante (de) in front
delicioso (-a/-os/-as) delicious
demasiado too, too much
demasiado (-a/-os/-as) too much,
  too many
depender to depend
(el/la) **dependiente/a**
  shop assistant
(el) **deporte** sport
derecho right (direction)
(el) **desastre** disaster
(el) **desayuno** breakfast

descansar to rest
describir to describe
desde from
desear to wish, to want
despacio slowly
(el) despacho office
despertar(se) to wake up
despedir to dismiss
despedirse to say goodbye
después (de) after
detrás (de) behind
devolver to return,
   to give back
(el) día day
(el) día libre day off
diciembre December
difícil difficult
dificultad difficulty
diligentemente diligently
(el) dinero money
directamente directly
(el) director / (la) directora
   director
(la) discusión argument
discutir to argue
dispuesto (-a/-os/-as) ready
divertido (-a/-os/-as) amusing
divertirse to have a good time
(el) documento document
(el) domingo Sunday
dormir to sleep
dormirse to go to sleep
(el) dormitorio bedroom
(la) ducha shower
dudar to doubt
dudoso (-a/-os/-as) doubtful
dulce sweet
durante during
durar to last

echar to throw, to pour
(el) edificio building
el the (m. sing.)
empezar to begin
(el/la) empleado/a employee
en in
enamorarse to fall in love

encantado (-a/-os/-as)
   delighted
encantador (-a/-os/-as) charming
encima (de) on top of
encontrar to find
encontrarse con to meet,
   to come across
enero January
enfadarse to get angry
enfermo (-a/-os/-as) ill
enfrente de in front of, opposite
enseñar to show, to teach
enterarse to find out
(el) entierro funeral
entonces then, in that case
entrar to come in
entre between
enviar to send
(el) equipaje luggage
(el) error error
escoger to choose
escribir to write
(el) escritorio desk
escuchar to listen
(la) escuela school
ese (-a/-os/-as) that, those
esforzarse to make an effort
España Spain
esperar to wait, to expect, to hope
espléndido (-a/-os/-as) generous,
   splendid, magnificent
esta noche tonight
(la) estación station, season
(el) estante shelf
estar to be (locations and
   temporary states)
estar en contacto con to be in
   touch with
este (-a/-os/-as) this, these
estudiar to study
(el/la) estudiante student
estupendo (-a/-os/-as) fantastic,
   great
estúpido (-a/-os/-as) stupid
(el) euro euro
(el) éxito success
(la) explicación explanation

(la) **fábrica** factory
fácil easy
fácilmente easily
faltar to lack, to be missing
famoso (-a/-os/-as) famous
(la) **farmacia** drugstore, pharmacy
febrero February
(la) **fecha** date
feliz happy
feo (-a/-os/-as) ugly
(la) **fiesta** party
fijarse en to notice
(la) **fila** line, row
(el) **fin** end
firmar to sign
(la) **flor** flower
(la) **fotografía** photograph
francés (francesa/-es/-as) French
(la) **fresa** strawberry
frecuentemente frequently
fresco (-a/-os/-as) fresh, cool
frío (-a/-os/-as) cold
(al) **fuego** (by the) fire
fuerte strong
fuerza de voluntad willpower
fumar to smoke
(la) **función** performance

(las) **gafas** glasses, spectacles
(la) **galleta** biscuit
ganar to earn, to win
(la) **gasolina** gas
(el) **gasto** expense
(el) **gato** cat
generalmente usually
(la) **gente** people
(el/la) **gerente** manager
(la) **ginebra** gin
(tener) **gracia** to be funny
gracias thanks
grande big
grave serious, grave
gritar to shout
(el) **guante** glove
guardar to keep
(el/la) **guardia** police officer

(la) **guerra** war
guisar to cook
gustar to like, to appeal to
(el) **gusto** pleasure, taste

haber to have (aux. verb)
(la) **habitación** room
hablar to speak, to talk
hacer to do, to make
hacer la maleta to pack (suitcase)
hacia toward
(el) **hambre** hunger
(la) **harina** flour
hasta until
(el) **helado** ice cream
helar to freeze
heredar to inherit
(la) **herida** injury
(el/la) **hermano/a** brother/sister
(el/la) **hijo/a** son/daughter
(la) **historia** history
hola hello
holgazán (holagazana/-es/-as) lazy
(el) **hombre** man
(la) **hora** hour, time (of the day)
(la) **hora de comer** lunchtime
horrible horrible
(el) **hospital** hospital
(el) **hotel** hotel
hoy today
hoy día nowadays
(el) **huevo** egg
huir to run away

(la) **idea** idea
(el) **idioma** language
(la) **iglesia** church
(las) **ilustraciones** illustrations
importante important
importar to matter
inaugurar to inaugurate
increíble incredible
inglés (inglesa/-es/-as) English
insistir to insist
insoportable unbearable
(las) **instrucciones** instructions
insultar to insult

inteligente intelligent
intentar to try to
interesante interesting
interesar to interest
(el) invierno winter
invitar to invite
ir to go
ir de compras to go shopping
ir de vacaciones to go on vacation
irse to go away
italiano (-a/-os/-as) Italian

jamás never
(el) jardín garden
(el) jerez sherry
joven young
(el) jueves Thursday
(el/la) juez judge
jugar to play
jugar (a) to play a game
julio July
junio June
juntos together
justo (-a/-os/-as) just, fair

(el) kilómetro kilometer

la the (f. sing.)
(el) ladrón / (la) ladrona thief
(el) lápiz pencil
largo (-a/-os/-as) long
(la) lástima pity, shame
lavar to wash
lavarse to wash oneself
(la) leche milk
leer to read
lejos far
lento (-a/-os/-as) slow
levantarse to get up
leve minor
(la) ley law
libre free (available)
(el) libro book
listo (-a/-os/-as) clever
Londres London
los / las the (m. pl. / f. pl.)
(el) lugar place

(el) lunes Monday
(la) luz light
llamar to call
llamarse to call oneself, to be called
(la) llave key
llegar to arrive
lleno (-a/-os/-as) full
llevar to wear, to carry
llevarse to take away
llorar to cry
llover to rain

(la) madre mother
mal badly
(la) maleta suitcase
(el) maletero car trunk
mandar to order
(la) manifestación demonstration
(la) mano hand
(la) manzana apple
mañana tomorrow
(el) mapa map
(la) máquina machine
(el) mar sea
maravillosamente wonderfully
(el) marido husband
(el) marisco seafood
(el) martes Tuesday
marzo March
más more
más tiempo longer
mayo May
(la) medianoche midnight
(el/la) médico/a doctor
medio (-a/-os/-as) half
mejor better
mejorar to get better
(el) melocotón peach
menos less
(el) mercado market
(el) mes month
(la) mesa table
meter to put in
mientras while
(el) miércoles Wednesday
mirar to look
mismo (-a/-os/-as) same

mojarse to get wet
molestar to bother, to trouble
(el) momento moment
(la) montaña mountain
montar en bicicleta to ride a bicycle
morder to bite
morir(se) to die
(el) motor engine, motor
mover to move
(el/la) muchacho/a boy/girl
mucho much, a lot
mucho (-a/-os/-as) much, a lot, many
muerto (-a/-os/-as) dead
(la) mujer wife, woman
(la) multa fine (penalty)
(el) museo museum
(la) música music
muy very

nada nothing
(el) nadador / (la) nadadora swimmer
nadie no one, nobody
(la) naranja orange
(la) neblina mist
necesitar to need
negro (-a/-os/-as) black
nevar to snow
ni ... ni neither ... nor
(la) niebla fog
(la) nieve snow
ninguno (-a/-os/-as) none
(el/la) niño/a boy/girl
(el) nombre name
(el) norte north
(la) noticia news
(la) novela novel
noviembre November
nuevo (-a/-os/-as) new
(el) número number
nunca never

o or
o ... o either ... or
obedecer to obey
(la) obra (de teatro) play

octavo (-a/-os/-as) eighth
octubre October
ocupado (-a/-os/-as) occupied, taken, busy
ocuparse de to attend to
ocurrir to happen
odiar to hate
odiarse to hate each other
(la) oficina office
ofrecer to offer
oír to hear
(el) olor smell
olvidar(se) to forget
(el) ordenador (portátil) computer (laptop)
(el) oro gold
(el) otoño autumn
otro (-a/-os/-as) other

(la) paciencia patience
(el) padre father
(los) padres parents
pagar to pay
(la) palabra word
(el) pan bread
(la) panadería bakery
(el) panecillo bread roll
(los) pantalones pants
(el) paquete parcel, package
para for
(la) parada de autobús bus stop
(el) paraguas umbrella
parar(se) to stop
parecer to seem
(los) parientes relatives
pasado (-a/-os/-as) past, last
pasar to spend (time), to pass
(la) pastilla pill, tablet
pedir to ask for, to order
pegar to hit
(la) película film
peligroso (-a/-os/-as) dangerous
(la) pelota ball
pensar to think
peor worse
pequeño (-a/-os/-as) small, little
perder to lose, to miss (train, boat)

perderse to lose one's way
perdonar to forgive
(el) periódico newspaper
permitir to allow
pero but
(el) perro dog
(la) persona person
pertenecer to belong
(el) pescado fish (as food)
(el) pez fish (animal)
(el) piano piano
(el) pie foot
(la) pierna leg
pintar to paint
(el) pintor / (la) pintora painter
(la) piscina swimming pool
(el) piso floor, flat (apartment)
(la) playa beach
(la) pluma pen
pobre poor
poco little (amount)
poco (-a/-os/-as) little, few
poder to be able to, can
(la) policía police
(el/la) policía police officer
poner to put
poner la mesa to lay/set the table
ponerse to put on
por by, along
(la) posibilidad possibility
(la) práctica practice
(el) precio price
preguntar to ask
(el) premio prize
preocuparse to worry
preparar to prepare
presentar to introduce
presentarse to appear, turn up
(el/la) presidente/a president
prestar to lend
(el/la) primo/a cousin
(la) primavera spring (season)
primero (-a/-os/-as) first
principal main
(el) principio beginning
probar to try, to test
(el) problema problem

(el) profesor / (la) profesora teacher
(el) programa program
prohibir to forbid
prometer to promise
pronto soon
(la) propina tip, gratuity
provocar to provoke
próximo (-a/-os/-as) next
publicado (-a/-os/-as) published
(el) pueblo village
(la) puerta door
(la) pulsera bracelet

que what, who, which, that
quedar to remain, to have left
quedarse to stay
quejarse to complain
querer to want, to love
quererse to love each other
quien who, whom
¿quién? who?, whom?
(las) quinielas football pools
quinto (-a/-os/-as) fifth
quitar to take away, remove
quitarse to take off (clothes)
quizá(s) perhaps

rápido (-a/-os/-as) fast
(la) razón reason
razonable reasonable
(la) rebaja reduction
(el) recado message
recibir to receive
recoger to pick up
recordar to remember
(el) regalo present
(la) reina queen
reírse to laugh
(el) reloj watch, clock
(la) representación performance
reservar to book
(el) resultado result
(el) retraso delay
(la) reunión meeting
(la) revista magazine
(el) rey king

rico (-a/-os/-as) rich, wealthy
(el) río river
(el) robo theft
romper(se) to break
ronco (-a/-os/-as) hoarse
(la) ropa clothes
roto (-a/-os/-as) broken
(el) ruido noise
ruso (-a/-os/-as) Russian

(el) sábado Saturday
saber to know (how or a fact)
saber a to taste of
(el) sacrificio sacrifice
salir to go out, to leave
(el) salón living room, lounge
saludar to greet
secar to dry
secarse to dry oneself
seco (-a/-os/-as) dry
(la) sed thirst
(la) seda silk
seguir to follow, to continue
según according to
segundo (-a/-os/-as) second
(el) sello postage stamp
(la) semana week
semejante such
sentarse to sit down
sentirse to feel
(las) señas address
(el) señor sir, Mr., gentleman
(la) señora madam, Ms., lady
(la) señorita Miss, young lady
septiembre September
séptimo (-a/-os/-as) seventh
ser to be (unchanging characteristics)
(el) servicio service
servir to serve
severamente severely
sexto (-a/-os/-as) sixth
siempre always
(el) silencio silence
(la) silla chair
(el) sillín seat (bicycle), saddle
(el) sillón armchair

simpático (-a/-os/-as) nice, friendly
sin without
(el) sitio place
(la) situación situation
sobrar to have to spare
(el) sobre envelope
sobre on, upon, about
(el/la) sobrino/a nephew/niece
(el) sofá sofa
(el) sol sun
solamente only
(el/la) soldado soldier
soler to be in the habit of
solo only
(el) sombrero hat
sonar to sound, to ring
sonreír to smile
soñar to dream
(la) sopa soup
sorprender to surprise
(la) sortija ring
subir to go up, to bring up, to climb
(el) suelo ground, floor
(la) suerte luck
(el) supermercado supermarket

(el) tabaco tobacco
tal such
(la) talla size
también also
tampoco neither
tanto so much
tanto (-a/-os/-as) so much, so many
tardar to take time
tarde late
(la) tarde afternoon, evening
(la) tarjeta de crédito credit card
(la) tarjeta postal postcard
(la) taza cup
(el) té tea
(el) teatro theater
telefonear to phone, to call up
(el) teléfono (móvil) telephone (cell)
(la) televisión television
temprano early

tener to have, to possess
tener éxito to succeed
(el) tenis tennis
tercero (-a/-os/-as) third
terminar to finish
(la) terraza balcony, terrace
(el/la) tío/a uncle/aunt
(el) tiempo weather, time (general)
(la) tienda shop
tocar to touch, to play (an
   instrument)
todo all, everything
todo (-a/-os/-as) every, whole
todo el mundo everyone
todos los días every day
tomar to take, to have (food, drink)
(la) tónica tonic water
tonto (-a/-os/-as) silly
(la) tortilla omelet
trabajar to work
(el) trabajo job, work
traducir to translate
traer to bring
tras after (behind)
tratar (de) to try
(el) tren train
(el) tribunal law court
triste sad
triunfar to succeed
(el/la) turista tourist
tronar to thunder

un (-a/-os/-as) a, one, some
(la) universidad university
único only (thing)
usar to use
útil useful
(la) uva grape

(las) vacaciones vacation
vacilar to hesitate
¡Vale! All right!, OK!
valer to be worth
valer la pena to be worth it
varios (-as) several
(la) velocidad speed
vender to sell

venir to come
(la) ventana window
(la) ventanilla window (of car)
ver to see
verse to see each other
(el) verano summer
(la) verdad truth
verdadero (-a/-os/-as) true
verde green
(el) vestido dress
vestirse to get dressed
viajar to travel
(el) viaje trip, journey
viejo (-a/-os/-as) old
(el) viento wind
(el) viernes Friday
(el) vino wine
(el) violín violin
visitar to visit
vivir to live
volver to return, to go back
(la) voz voice

ya already
ya no no longer

(la) zapatería shoe store
(el) zapato shoe
(la) zona area
(el) zumo juice

In this section, (v.) is indicated for any English verbs that might otherwise be confused with nouns. The same goes for a few other parts of speech: nouns (n.), adjectives (a.), etc. In the Spanish definitions, an asterisk * indicates adjectives that change form according to gender/number; the masculine singular (or, where appropriate, the masculine plural) is shown.

a un, una
about sobre
accept aceptar
accident accidente
accompany acompañar
according to según
accountant contable (m. & f.)
accuse acusar
actor actor
actress actriz
address señas
advise aconsejar
after después (de)
after (behind) tras
afternoon tarde
against contra
airplane avión
airport aeropuerto
allow dejar(se), permitir
All right! ¡Vale!
almost casi
along por
a lot mucho*
already ya
also también
always siempre
amount cantidad
amusing divertido*
announce anunciar
answer (v.) contestar
any alguno*
anything cualquier cosa
apartment piso
aperitif aperitivo
appear presentarse
apple manzana
approach (v.) acercarse

April abril
architect arquitecto/a
area zona
argue discutir
argument discusión
arm brazo
armchair sillón
arrest (v.) arrestar
arrive llegar
as como
ask preguntar
ask for pedir
assist asistir
at a
attend asistir
attend to ocuparse de
aunt tía
autumn otoño

badly mal
bag bolsa
bakery panadería
balcony terraza
ball pelota
bank banco
bath (someone) (v.) bañar
bathe (oneself) bañarse
bathroom baño
be ser, estar
be able to poder
beach playa
bed cama
bedroom dormitorio
beer cerveza
before ante, antes de
begin empezar
beginning (n.) principio

behind detrás (de)
believe creer
belong pertenecer
better mejor
between entre
bicycle bicicleta
big grande*
bill (account) cuenta
bill (money) billete
birthday cumpleaños
biscuit galleta
bite (v.) morder
black negro*
blame (n.) culpa
blind (a.) ciego*
blue azul*
boat (rowing) barca
boat (ship) barco
book (v.) reservar
book libro
boring aburrido*
bother molestar
bottle botella
box caja
boy muchacho, niño
bracelet pulsera
brandy coñac
bread pan
bread roll panecillo
break romper, romperse
breakfast desayuno
bring traer
bring up(stairs) subir
broken roto*
brother hermano
build construir
building edificio
bullet bala
burglar ladrón / ladrona
bus autobús
bus stop parada de autobús
busy concurrido*, ocupado*
but pero
butcher's shop carnicería
buy comprar

call (v.) llamar
call oneself llamarse

call up telefonear
cancel cancelar
capital capital
car coche, automóvil
carry llevar
cat gato
cathedral catedral
celebrate celebrar
censor (v.) censurar
certain cierto
chair silla
change (n.) cambio
charge (v.) cobrar
charming encantador*
cheap barato*
check cheque
chocolates bombones
choose escoger
church iglesia
cigarette cigarrillo, pitillo
cinema cine
city ciudad
clever listo*
client cliente / clienta
climate clima
climb (v.) subir
clock reloj
close (v.) cerrar
clothes ropa
coach autocar
coast costa
coat abrigo
coffee café
coincidence casualidad
cold (a.) frío*
colleague compañero/a
color color
come venir
come across
    encontrarse con
come in entrar
companion compañero/a
complain quejarse
computer (laptop) ordenador
    (portátil)
concert concierto
consent (v.) consentir
conservative conservador*

contact contacto
content oneself contentarse
conversation conversación
cook (v.) cocinar, guisar
correct correcto*
cost (v.) costar
count (v.) contar
countryside campo
cousin primo/a
covered cubierto*
cry (v.) llorar
cup taza
cupboard armario
curiosity curiosidad
custom (habit) costumbre
Customs Aduana

damage daño
dance (v.) bailar
dance, dancing baile
dangerous peligroso*
date fecha
daughter hija
dawn (v.) amanecer
day día
day off día libre
dead muerto*
December diciembre
decide decidir(se)
delay (n.) retraso
delicious delicioso*
delighted encantado*
demonstration manifestación
depend depender
describe describir
desk escritorio
die morir, morirse
difficult difícil*
difficulty dificultad
diligently diligentemente
dine, have dinner cenar
dining room comedor
dinner cena
director director/directora
disaster desastre
disc disco
dismiss despedir
do hacer

doctor médico/a
document documento
dog perro
door puerta
doubt (v.) dudar
doubtful dudoso*
drawer cajón
dream (v.) soñar
dress vestido
drink bebida, aperitivo
drink (v.) beber
drink, to have a tomar una copa
drive (v.) conducir
dry seco*
dry (v.) secar
dry oneself secarse
during durante

each cada
early temprano
earn ganar
easily fácilmente
easy fácil*
eat comer
edge borde
egg huevo
eighth octavo*
either ... or o ... o
elevator ascensor
employee empleado/a
end fin
engine motor
English inglés*
enough bastante
enough, to be bastar
envelope sobre
error error
euro euro
evening tarde
every todo*
every day todos los días
everyone todo el mundo
everything todo
expect esperar
expense gasto
expensive caro*
explanation explicación

factory fábrica
fairly bastante
fall in love enamorarse
famous famoso*
fantastic estupendo*
far lejos
fast rápido*
father padre
fault culpa
February febrero
feel (v.) sentirse
few poco*
fifth quinto*
film película
find (v.) encontrar
find out enterarse
fine bien
fine (penalty) multa
finish (v.) acabar,
   terminar
fire, by the al fuego
first primero*
fish (food) pescado
fish (animal) pez
fit in(to) (v.) caber
floor suelo, piso
flour harina
flower flor
fog niebla
follow seguir
food comida
foot pie
for para
forbid prohibir
forget olvidar(se)
forgive perdonar
fourth cuarto*
free (available) libre*
free (of charge) gratuito*
freeze (v.) helar
French francés*
frequently frecuentemente
fresh fresco*
Friday viernes
friend amigo/a
friendly simpático*
from de, desde
full lleno*

funeral entierro
funny, to be tener gracia

garden jardín
gas gasolina
generous espléndido*
gentleman señor
German alemán*
get angry enfadarse
get better mejorar
get dark anochecer
get dressed vestirse
get married casarse
get tired cansarse
get up levantarse
get wet mojarse
gin ginebra
girl muchacha, chica, niña
give dar
give back devolver
glad, to be alegrarse
glasses (spectacles) gafas
glove guante
go ir
go away irse
go back volver
go down bajar
go for a walk dar un paseo
go on seguir
go on vacation ir de vacaciones
go out salir
go shopping ir de compras
go to bed acostarse
go to sleep dormirse
go up subir
gold oro
good bueno*
goodbye adiós
goodwill buena intención
grandfather/mother abuelo/a
grape uva
grave (serious) grave*
green verde*
greet saludar
ground (floor) suelo

habit costumbre
habit of, to be in the soler

half medio*
hand mano
handbag bolso
happen ocurrir
happy contento*, feliz*
hat sombrero
hate (v.) odiar
hate each other odiarse
have (aux. verb) haber
have (food/drink) tomar
have (possess) tener
have a good time divertirse
have left quedar
have to spare sobrar
hear oír
heat calor
hello hola
help (v.) ayudar
help each other ayudarse
helper ayudante (m. & f.)
hesitate vacilar
hill colina
hire (v.) alquilar
history historia
hit (v.) pegar
holidays vacaciones
home casa
hope (v.) esperar
horrible horrible*
horse caballo
hospital hospital
hot caliente*
hotel hotel
hoarse ronco*
hour hora
house casa
how como
how much cuánto
hunger hambre
husband marido
hurry (v.) darse prisa

ice cream helado
idea idea
ill enfermo*
illustration ilustración
immediately directamente
important importante*

in a, en
in front (of) delante (de)
in that case entonces
inaugurate inaugurar
incredible increíble*
inherit heredar
injury daño, herida
insist insistir
instructions instrucciones
insult (v.) insultar
insurance company compañía
   de seguros
intelligent inteligente*
interest (v.) interesar
interesting interesante*
introduce presentar
invite invitar
Italian italiano*

jacket chaqueta
January enero
job trabajo
journey viaje
judge juez (m. & f.)
July julio
June junio
just (fair) justo*

keep (v.) guardar
key llave
kilometer kilómetro
kind amable
king rey
kitchen cocina
know (how, a fact) saber
know (be acquainted with)
   conocer

lack (v.) faltar
lady señora
language idioma
last (past) pasado*
last (v.) durar
late tarde
laugh (v.) reírse
law ley
law court tribunal
lay/set the table poner la mesa

lazy holgazán*
lean out asomarse
learn aprender
leave behind dejar
leg pierna
lend prestar
less menos
let (v.) dejar
letter carta
light luz
like (v.) gustar
like como
line (queue) fila
listen escuchar
little pequeño*, poco*
little (amount) poco
live (v.) vivir
living room salón
London Londres
long largo*
longer más tiempo
look (v.) mirar
look after cuidar
look for buscar
lose perder
lose one's way perderse
lorry camión
lounge salón
love (v.) querer
love each other quererse
lovely bonito*, precioso*
luck suerte
luggage equipaje
lunch comida
lunchtime hora de comer

machine máquina
magazine revista
mail correo
main principal*
make hacer
make an effort esforzarse
man hombre
manage conseguir
manager gerente (m. & f.)
many muchos*
map mapa
March marzo

market mercado
married casado*
matches cerillas
matter (v.) importar
May mayo
meal comida
meat carne
meet (v.) encontrarse con
message recado
midnight medianoche
milk leche
minor leve*
Miss señorita
miss (train, etc.) perder
missing, to be faltar
mist neblina
moment momento
Monday lunes
money dinero
month mes
more más
mother madre
motor motor
mountain montaña
move (v.) mover
Mr./Mrs. señor / señora
much mucho*
museum museo
music música
must deber

name nombre
near cerca
necklace collar
necktie corbata
need (v.) necesitar
neither tampoco
neither … nor ni … ni
nephew sobrino
never jamás, nunca
new nuevo*
news noticia
newspaper periódico
next próximo*
nice simpático*
niece sobrina
nightgown camisón
noise ruido

no longer ya no
none ninguno*
no one nadie
north norte
nothing nada
notice (v.) fijarse en
novel novela
November noviembre
now ahora
nowadays hoy día
number número

obey obedecer
obtain conseguir
occupied ocupado*
October octubre
of de
of course claro
offer (v.) ofrecer
office despacho, oficina
often a menudo
OK! ¡Vale!
old viejo*
omelet tortilla
on sobre
one uno*
only solamente, solo
only (thing) único
on top of encima
open (v.) abrir
opposite enfrente de
or o
orange (n.) naranja
order (v.) mandar, pedir
other otro*
owe deber

pack (v.) (suitcase) hacer la
  maleta
paint (v.) pintar
painter pintor / pintora
painting (picture) cuadro
parcel paquete
parents padres
parking lot aparcamiento
party fiesta
pass (v.) pasar
past pasado*

patience paciencia
pay (v.) pagar
peach melocotón
pen pluma
pencil lápiz
people gente
performance función,
  representación
perhaps acaso, quizás
person persona
pharmacy farmacia
photograph fotografía
piano piano
pick up (v.) recoger
picture (painting) cuadro
pill pastilla
pity lástima
place (n.) lugar, sitio
play (theater) obra (de teatro)
play (v.) jugar
play (an instrument) tocar
pleasant agradable*
pleased contento*
pleasure gusto
pocket bolsillo
police policía
police officer guardia, policía
  (m. & f.)
poor pobre*
possibility posibilidad
postcard (tarjeta) postal
postage stamp sello
practice práctica
prepare preparar
present (n.) regalo
president presidente/a
pretty bonito*
price precio
prize premio
problem problema
promise (v.) prometer
provoke provocar
published publicado*
punish castigar
purchases compras
put poner
put in meter
put on ponerse

quarter cuarto
queen reina
quiet, to be callarse

rain (v.) llover
read leer
ready dispuesto*
reason razón
reasonable razonable*
receive recibir
reduction rebaja
relatives parientes
remain quedar
remember acordarse (de), recordar
rest (v.) descansar
result resultado
return (v.) volver, devolver
rich rico*
ride a bike montar en bicicleta
right (correct) correcto*
right (direction) derecho*
ring (v.) (bell, etc.) sonar
ring (on finger) anillo, sortija
river río
road carretera
room cuarto, habitación
row (line) fila
rowboat barca
run away huir
Russian ruso*

sacrifice sacrificio
sad triste
saddle (bicycle) sillín
same mismo*
sandwich bocadillo
Saturday sábado
save (money) ahorrar
say (v.) decir
say goodbye despedirse
school escuela, colegio
sea mar
seafood marisco
season estación
seat asiento
second segundo*
see ver
see each other verse

seem parecer
seize apresar
sell vender
send enviar
September septiembre
serious grave*
serve (v.) servir
service servicio
seventh séptimo*
several varios*
severely severamente
shelf estante
sherry jerez
ship barco
shirt camisa
shoe zapato
shoe store zapatería
shoot (v.) disparar
shop tienda
shop assistant dependiente/a
shopping compras
shout (v.) gritar
show (v.) enseñar
shower ducha
sign (v.) firmar
silence silencio
silk seda
silly tonto*
sing cantar
sir señor
sister hermana
sit down sentarse
situation situación
sixth sexto*
size talla
sleep (v.) dormir, dormirse
slow lento*
slowly despacio
small pequeño*
smell (n.) olor
smile (v.) sonreír
smoke (v.) fumar
snow nieve
snow (v.) nevar
so así (que)
so many tantos*
so much tanto, tanto*
sofa sofá

soldier soldado (m. & f.)
some unos, unas
some (any) alguno*
someone alguien
something algo
son hijo
soon pronto
sound (v.) sonar
soup sopa
sour agrio*
Spain España
speak hablar
spectacles gafas
speed velocidad
spend (time) pasar
sport deporte
spring (season) primavera
start (a car) arrancar
station estación
stay (v.) quedarse
stop (v.) parar, pararse
strawberry fresa
street calle
strong fuerte*
student alumno/a,
  estudiante (m. & f.)
study (v.) estudiar
stupid estúpido*
succeed tener éxito, triunfar
success éxito
such tal, semejante*
suffice bastar
sugar azúcar
suitcase maleta
summer verano
sun sol
Sunday domingo
supermarket supermercado
surprise (v.) sorprender
sweet dulce*
swimmer nadador / nadadora
swimming pool piscina

table mesa
take tomar
take away llevarse, quitar
taken ocupado*
take off (clothes) quitarse

take time tardar
talk (v.) hablar
tall alto*
taste of saber a
tea té
teach enseñar
teacher profesor / profesora
telephone (mobile) teléfono
  (móvil)
telephone (v.) telefonear
television televisión
tennis tenis
tenth décimo*
terrace terraza
test (v.) probar
thanks gracias
that ese*, que
that (over there) aquel*
the el, los, la, las
theater teatro
theft robo
then entonces
there allí
there is/are hay
these estos*
thief ladrón / ladrona
thing cosa
think pensar
third tercero*
thirst sed
this este*
those esos*
those (over there) aquellos*
threaten amenazar
thunder (v.) tronar
Thursday jueves
thus así (que)
ticket billete
tie (neck) corbata
time (general) tiempo
time (of the day) hora
tip (gratuity) propina
tired cansado*
to a
tobacco tabaco
today hoy
together juntos*
tomorrow mañana

too (much) demasiado
touch (v.) tocar
tourist turista (m. & f.)
toward hacia
town ciudad
train tren
translate traducir
travel (v.) viajar
tree árbol
trip (journey) viaje
trouble (v.) molestar
trousers pantalones
true verdadero*
trunk (of car) maletero
truth verdad
try probar, tratar (de)
try to intentar
Tuesday martes

ugly feo*
umbrella paraguas
unbearable insoportable*
uncle tío
under bajo
underneath debajo (de)
understand comprender
understand each other
  comprenderse
university universidad
until hasta
upon sobre
upstairs arriba
use (v.) usar
useful útil*
usually generalmente

very muy
village pueblo
violin violín
visit (v.) visitar
voice voz

wait (v.) esperar
waiter camarero/a
wake up despertar(se)
walk (v.) andar
want (v.) desear, querer
war guerra

wardrobe armario
warn avisar
warning (sign) aviso
wash (v.) lavar
wash (oneself) lavarse
watch reloj
water agua
way (road) camino
wear (v.) llevar
wealthy rico*
weather tiempo
wedding boda
Wednesday miércoles
week semana
well (good) bien
what que
when cuando
where to adonde
which cual, que
while mientras
white blanco*
who que, quien, ¿quién?
whom quien, ¿quién?
wife mujer
willpower fuerza de
  voluntad
win (v.) ganar
wind viento
window ventana
window (of car) ventanilla
wine vino
winter invierno
wish (v.) desear
with con
without sin
woman mujer
wonderfully maravillosamente
word palabra
work (n.) trabajo
work (v.) trabajar
worry (v.) preocuparse
worth (to be) valer
worse peor
write escribir

year año
young joven*

Index

The numbers refer to sections, not pages.

"a," "an" 1.1, 9.12
Adjectives:
  agreement 2.3
  demonstrative 3.1
  gender of 2.3
  plural of 2.3
  position of 8.2
  possessive 4.1
  shortening of 8.1
Adverbs 7.5
Articles:
  definite (the) 1.1, 2.1, 9.12
  indefinite (a, an) 1.1,
    2.1, 9.12
Augmentative 13.6

"to be" 2.4–2.6

Comparison 7.6–7.9
Conditional 8.7–8.9

Dates 4.9
Days of the week 4.6
deber ("must") 11.1
Definite article 1.1, 9.12
Demonstrative adjectives
  and pronouns 3.1–3.2
Diminutives 13.6

"either/or" 7.4
estar 2.4, 2.6
Exclamations 6.2

Familiar/polite form 1.4
Forms of address 1.4–1.5
Future tense 8.5–8.6, 8.9

"to go" (**ir**) 5.1
gustar 6.10

hacer, idiomatic uses of 6.8
"to have" aux. verb (**haber**)
  5.3–5.4, 7.1, 7.3
"to have" (**tener**) 1.6
hay 5.4

"If" clauses 12.5
Imperative form
  (familiar) 11.6
  (polite) 5.9
Imperfect (tense) 7.1, 9.6
Imperfect subjunctive 12.1,
  12.3
Impersonal verbs 6.9
Indefinite article 1.1, 9.12
ir ("to go") 5.1

"to know" (**conocer/saber**)
  9.7

más … de, menos … de
  13.2
más … que, menos … que
  7.9
Months 4.7

Negative, forming 1.7
  "never," "nothing," etc. 7.4
Nouns:
  gender of 1.2
  plural of 1.3
Numbers (cardinal) 4.3
  (ordinal) 4.4

Passive voice 10.2–10.3
Past participle 5.2, 8.4
  used with **ser** to form
  passive 2.5
Past perfect 7.3

Past perfect subjunctive 12.2–12.3
pero and sino 13.4
Personal a 5.5
Possession 2.2
Possessive adjectives 4.1
  possessive pronouns 4.2
Prepositions 8.10, 10.5, 12.8, 13.5
  por and para 10.1
Present (tense) 3.3, 6.3, 6.7, 7.7, 8.3
Present continuous 3.4
Present participle 3.4
Present perfect 5.3
  subjunctive 11.4
Present subjunctive 11.3
Preterit tense 9.1–9.6
Pronouns:
  demonstrative 3.1
  disjunctive (stressed) 6.6
  interrogative 3.5
  personal (object) 5.6–5.8
  personal (subject) 1.4
  possessive 4.2
  reflexive 6.4
  relative 3.6

querer 6.11
Questions, forming 1.8, 6.1
  question words 3.5, 6.1

Reflexive verbs/pronouns 6.4
  reciprocal form 6.5
Regular verbs 3.3
Relative pronouns 3.6

saber and poder ("can") 11.2
Seasons 4.8
seguir, idiomatic uses of 11.7

ser 2.4–2.5
soler (used to) 7.2
"some" 1.1
Spelling changes in verbs 10.4
Subject pronouns 1.4
Subjunctive 11.3–11.5, 12.1–12.6
Superlatives 9.8–9.10

tan and tal 13.3
tener ("to have") 1.6
  idiomatic uses of 1.9
"the" 1.1, 9.12
"this," "that" 3.2
Time 4.5

valer, idiomatic uses of 11.8
Verbs:
  conditional 8.7–8.9
  followed by an infinitive 10.5
  followed by a preposition 12.8
  future tense 8.5–8.6, 8.9
  imperative (polite) 5.9
  impersonal 6.9
  passive 10.2–10.3
  past participle 5.2, 8.4
  past perfect 7.3
  present participle 3.4
  present perfect 5.3
  present tense 3.3, 6.7, 8.3
  preterite tense 9.1–9.6
  reciprocal form 6.5
  reflexive 6.4
  regular (introduction) 3.3
  spelling changes 10.4
  stem-changing 6.3
  subjunctive 11.3–11.5, 12.1–12.6

"what," "which," "who," etc. 3.5–3.6